WHITETAIL!

North America's Top Deer Hunters
Share Their Strategies And Secrets

SHADY OAK PRESS

About the Editor

Though hunting season may take Gregg Gutschow from the alpine peaks of mountain goat country to the plains of antelope country and everywhere in between, the whitetail—and whitetail hunting—captures his heart and soul. He knows the deer, he knows hunting them ... and he knows who today's top hunters are. Discover their secrets in this one-of-kind hunting volume.

WHITETAIL!

North America's Top Deer Hunters
Share Their Strategies And Secrets

Tom Carpenter
Creative Director

Jen Weaverling
Production Editor

Heather Koshiol
Book Development Coordinator

Julie Cisler, Greg Schwieters
Book Design and Production

David Rottinghaus
Commissioned Illustrations

Phil Aarrestad
Commissioned Photography

Donald M. Jones
Front and Back Cover Photography

1 2 3 4 5 6 / 12 11 10 09 08 07
ISBN 978-1-58159-319-8
© 1998 North American Membership Group

Distributed by:
Sterling Publishing Co., Inc.
387 Park Avenue South
New York, NY 10016-8810

For information about custom editions, special sales, premium and corporate purchases, please contact Sterling Special Sales Department at 800-805-5489 or specialsales@sterlingpub.com.

PHOTO CREDITS

Charles Alsheimer: 17, 30, 32, 63, 65, 66, 70, 75, 76, 77 (top), 78, 92, 96, 105, 107; **Grady Allen:** 123; **Brian P. Bower:** 116, 133; **Denver Bryan:** 12; **Bill Buckley/THE GREEN AGENCY:** 38; **Tim Christie:** 8-9, 36-37, 41, 45, 86, 101; **Gary Clancy:** 44, 97, 98, 132; **Judd Cooney:** 48, 50, 52, 53, 57, 111, 152, 155; **Jeanne Drake:** 21; **Tom Fegely:** 120, 121; **John Ford:** 16, 28; **Michael H. Francis:** 1, 60; **Donald M. Jones:** 77 (bottom), 117, covers; **Mark Kayser:** 59, 68-69, 71, 126, 144; **Bill Kinney:** 22, 29, 95, 112-113, 114, 124, 127, 129, 130, 146, 165; **Lance Kreuger:** 19, 20, 23, 62, 83, 85, 108, 142, 156, 158, 159; **Lon E. Lauber:** 27, 31, 89, 102, 148; **Bill Lea:** 14, 15, 40, 94; **Bill Marchel:** 61, 82, 106, 109, 115, 125, 131, 143, 147, 170; **Steve Maslowski:** 64; **Mark Raycroft:** 4, 6-7, 67, 100, 119, 150-151; **Jim Shockey:** 135-141; **Ron Spomer:** 110, 145; **Bill Vaznis/THE GREEN AGENCY:** 154; **Wensel Bros.:** 39; **Beth Winke:** 79; **Bill Winke:** 73, 74 (bottom), 80, 103, 162, 168; **John Wootters:** 171. Remaining photographs property of NAMG: 18, 24, 43, 46, 47, 49, 51, 58, 74 (top), 90, 81, 84, 87, 93, 104, 128, 164, 166.

SHADY OAK PRESS
12301 Whitewater Drive
Minnetonka, MN 55343

Table of Contents

CHAPTER FIVE
Persistence Pays 150

INDEX

Foreword

While it's true that there is an element of luck involved with deer hunting, it's also true that most of that luck is earned.

Yes, we've all heard about the first-time hunter that shoots the biggest buck in the county that year. Or the opening weekend warrior that stumbles upon a breathtaking buck that makes one of the record books.

But that's not most of us. Most of us are regular people who have to put in our time to achieve our hunting goals. And there's nothing wrong with that: Just being out there hunting is most of the journey's reward.

But whether you want to tag a mature buck, get your biggest buck yet, shoot any buck at all, or put some fine venison on the table with antlerless deer … and those are all perfectly fine and respectable goals … the way to success is through effort and knowledge.

We can't help you with the effort part, yet I'm betting you have the commitment to hunt hard. But we can help you with the knowledge part — hunting smart — and that's where *WHITETAIL!* comes in. I invite you to come along as *North America's Top Deer Hunters Share Their Strategies and Secrets.*

Jim Shockey, Judd Cooney, David Morris, Charles Alsheimer, Gene and Barry Wensel, John Wootters, Bill Winke and editor Gregg Gutschow … the contributors to these pages truly do represent the best, brightest and most passionate of North America's white-tailed deer hunters. They will help you understand whitetails better, scout and plan more intelligently, hunt more effectively, find big old bucks (and who doesn't like a big old buck now and again?), and motivate you to hunt with a positive frame of mind.

It's true. You earn your own luck — by knowing deer, by hunting with a plan, and by hunting hard. It's a simple formula. But it works. It's time to let these experts give you some ideas for the whitetail trail.

Tom

Tom Carpenter
Shady Oak Press

Introduction

*I*s there really such a thing as an *expert* deer hunter? Though some men and women possess mountains of experience and forests full of woodsmanship, most of us humans are not incredibly predatory. Wolves are expert hunters.

Whitetails humble human hunters more than any other big game animal. Maybe that's why we're in awe of the handful of hunters who have a knack for notching tags consistently ... on old bucks.

That's the kind of hunter who contributed to this book. We've called them "pros" to title this excellent collection of deer hunting insight. And they certainly all are professionals since most of them make all or a good chunk of their income from communicating whitetail hunting know-how to others.

Think about all the hours you spend at work. Now imagine that you spend the same amount of time—and more—studying and pursuing whitetails. Many of these writers have been at it like this for 20 years or more. Okay, maybe we *could* call them experts. But each one would probably cringe if publicly introduced as a "whitetail hunting expert." Why? Because like any of us, they spend the vast majority of their hunting days watching the whitetails come out on top.

But you, the reader, are the beneficiary of these pros' deer hunting days—good and bad. In this book we get a chance to see inside all that experience. It is a rare opportunity to gather so much talent in one place. So, just like you would do if you were in deer camp with some of these hunters, now is a good time to sit back and just listen.

Chapter 1

A UNIQUE ANIMAL

One big game animal stands head and shoulders above all others in a popularity contest with hunters in North America. You're right, it's the whitetail. Something like 80 percent of us hunt this fascinating creature.

One might jump to the conclusion that this statistic is simply a function of the deer's incredible range, which stretches from Mexico well into Canada, and from Washington state to Maine. Most of us have whitetails outside our back door. Or what about some of the long seasons stretching from August to late January? Or the liberal bag limits per season in some states?

All this surely plays a role in the whitetail's popularity.

But what about the way a whitetail buck sometimes charges to rattling horns or a grunt call? What about the way he thrusts his chin high into the breeze and rolls his head side to side, testing the air currents for human scent or the smell of a hot doe? What about how he calmly crunches acorns one second and tenses on all-out full alert the next? And what about how he makes the most veteran deer hunter quake even on a warm day? What about all that?

Those are the real reasons for our connection with whitetails. Let's hope that it does not happen, but even if sometime during our lifetimes white-tailed deer numbers dip, or their range contracts, whitetails will still be whitetails and deer hunters will still be deer hunters. We'll still hit the woods with an extra beat in our hearts and a little sweat on our palms.

This chapter is about introduction. David Morris kicks it off in fine fashion with "Why We Love It." Then John Wootters tells us more about what makes whitetails tick.

And then you'll discover ...

WHY WE LOVE IT

by David Morris

*T*he thought, "What manner of animal is this?" probably first formed in my mind on a cold, windy afternoon in Georgia during the very early years of my hunting career. I already had several small- and a couple of medium-sized bucks to my credit, but a really big buck still eluded me.

In the process of accompanying my wife to her treestand high on a hill overlooking a recently harvested soybean field, I cast a casual glance toward another large bean field several hundred yards to my left. Much to my surprise, a whopper buck was nervously trotting down a narrow hedgerow winding through the middle of the field. Excitement got the best of me, and I foolishly hurried a couple of absurdly long shots into the teeth of a 30 mph crosswind. Due to the wind and the distance, the buck had no idea where the shots came from, and I had no idea where they went. Uncertain of the danger, the buck ducked into the thin cover of the hedgerow and miraculously disappeared. Rifle ready, I waited several minutes for the buck to show himself in the skimpy hedgerow, but nothing not pushed by the wind moved.

Turning to my wife, I shouted above the wind, "He bedded down in the hedgerow. I'm going after him. Stay here and watch for him. Signal me if you see him."

With that, I departed quickly for the hedgerow, checking back occasionally for a sign from

You never have a whitetail buck dead-to-rights. He'll hide, leap, sprint, juke, crawl and even hold his breath ... anything to survive.

my wife but receiving nothing more than a shoulder shrug. When I reached the hedgerow, I began my slow stalk, rifle at port arms. I entered the hedgerow well above where the buck had disappeared, assured by my wife that he was still somewhere in that thin ribbon of brush. As I eased along, I began to doubt that a 200-pound buck with that much bone on his head could possibly hide in the scant cover afforded by the carpet of honeysuckle vines and the scattered persimmon and honey locust trees that made up the hedgerow. The farther I went, the more skeptical I became, despite my wife's assurance that the buck had not left the hedgerow.

Upon reaching the point where the buck had vanished, a shallow, honeysuckle-choked drainage ditch began to run through the center of the hedgerow, forcing me to proceed along the edge rather than the center. Looking ahead, I could see that the hedgerow wound another 100 yards before petering out, leaving only the broomsedge and honeysuckle-rimmed ditch to make its way to the thick pines some 75 yards farther on. If the buck was still around, and all evidence said that he was, he had to be between me and the end of the hedgerow.

I proceeded on red alert but not without considerable skepticism. Yard after yard, nothing. Not even an obvious place for a buck to hide. Frequent checks with my wife assured me that the buck had not slipped out, at least not via any visible route. I continued down the left side of the hedgerow until only 15 yards remained. Still no sign of the buck. I had all but given up when the ground in front of me erupted into a huge buck. No time to marvel over where he had come from. Time to act!

The big buck immediately put the hedgerow between him and me, and I immediately set sail to remedy that. Brimming with anticipation, I knew I had him. With me right on his tail, there was no way the buck could cross that wide-open 75 yards to the woods without me getting off two or three good shots.

"He had pulled off an impossible escape and denied me his presence on my wall when I had him cold!"

I burst forth from the hedgerow, head snapping left and right, ready to shoot—but the buck was nowhere to be seen. Frantic, I ran forward 10 yards for a better view. The soybean field remained empty. Desperate, I turned to my wife on the far hill for help. Upon seeing me look her way, she held both arms straight in front of her and began pointing frantically toward the ground. Precious seconds passing, my mind raced. The ground? He went to the ground? Then it hit me. The ditch!

Even as I raced toward the ditch, my eyes futilely traced its course to the woods. Refusing to believe that the buck had gotten away so completely unscathed, I half expected to find him burrowed up somewhere in the three-foot crevice as I ran alongside it for several yards. But alas, the tracks told the story, almost as clearly as my wife did later on!

The buck had indeed escaped down the ditch. Deep, splayed, running tracks marred the full length of the silty ditch bottom. His escape was so slick and completely undetected, at least by me, that I first believed he must have belly-crawled that 75 yards. But his far-apart tracks told me that wasn't so, as did my wife who had observed it all through binoculars from her elevated vantage point. Hugging the ground, he had run flat out down that ditch, his well-adorned head held low and outstretched. He had pulled off an impossible escape and denied me his presence on my wall when I had him cold! As I stood there and looked at those tracks, the thought first hit me, "What manner of animal is this?"

LIVING WITH DEER

by John Wootters

W hite-tailed deer are known as the most sedentary of all North American big game animals. In some areas (northern Michigan, for example) an individual deer might live out its whole life within a home range as small as 500 acres. Large geographic differences do exist, however. Telemetry of mature bucks in the south Texas brush country has shown that some of them might ramble over 4,000 acres or more. Generally, the more lush the habitat and/or the smaller the population, the more limited the home ranges of individual animals. Everywhere, does are noticeably more likely than bucks to remain close to their birthplaces.

DEFINING RANGE AND TERRITORY

The term "home range" is not synonymous with "territory." A territory, in biologists' lingo, is an area defended by its occupant against other individuals of the same species. A home range is simply a definable area where an animal spends most of its time, and a home range might be occupied simultaneously by other individuals. By these definitions, white-tailed deer are not truly territorial creatures. Their attachment to their home ranges, however, is so strong that it is almost impossible to drive a whitetail out of its own turf permanently with anything less than fire or bulldozers.

Attachment to home is one of the whitetail's most effective defenses against hunters, allowing the deer to be intimately familiar with every feature of a small chunk of terrain—and believe me, they are! It might be an exaggeration to say that a deer literally knows the appearance of every shrub in its range from every angle, but it's not too much to say that it is familiar enough with the landforms and vegetation patterns to be very quick to notice something new. Any hunter who has ever tried to sneak a new blind into whitetail country, hoping to be ignored, knows that.

Some years ago I owned a ranch in East Texas on which I raised cattle and hunted whitetails. Like most landowners, I put out blocks of mineralized salt for the livestock, always placing them in the same exact spots around the woodland pasture. One block, which I could see from one of my hunting stands, had been depleted for a couple of weeks before I got around to dropping off a fresh one, which I did on my way to that stand one afternoon during deer season.

Just before dark, a few does and fawns were feeding in the opening when one of the fawns noticed the new salt block. That little deer had a fit—snorting, dancing around, flagging and generally raising such a fuss that it made its mother too nervous to continue feeding. The new object in the young deer's environment instantly caught its attention and made it suspicious, even though a block of exactly the same color, size and shape had occupied the identical spot until a week or two prior to this episode.

—◦◦◦—

"This sensitivity to alterations in, and fondness for, their home ranges is perhaps the most distinctive of all whitetail characteristics."

—◦◦◦—

This sensitivity to alterations in, and fondness for, their home ranges is perhaps the most distinctive of all whitetail characteristics. This valuable characteristic permits the hunter to hunt one specific animal over and over again. The whitetail is the only big game species that a hunter can assume will remain within a defined area more or less indefinitely, year-round. If a deer was there yesterday, chances are good that it will be there tomorrow, next week and even next year.

You might not be able to find it anytime you wish, but you can be pretty sure it's there somewhere. You can hunt a deer today and miss, then try again in a few days with some confidence that it will be available for a rematch. Specific bucks are often hunted year after year, being glimpsed

repeatedly in a given area and sometimes gaining considerable local fame. Some acquire nicknames and, eventually, personal legends. That all this can be true while mature bucks remain so difficult to take is an impressive testimony to their survival skills!

In any case, whatever activity a whitetail might engage in and whatever makes it move, that movement will probably be confined within a relatively small area—the deer's familiar, beloved home range.

Sometimes whitetail bucks seem to be creatures of habit. Other times a buck will appear exactly where we least expect him to.

ANNUAL CYCLES

White-tailed deer, like all mammals, live their lives according to certain annual cycles which are driven by seasonal changes in the weather and habitat, hormonal changes in their own bodies and other long-term factors. The impact of these cycles on deer activity is often inconspicuous to the casual observer or to one who watches a deer herd during a single part of the year (such as hunting season only).

Deer movement to winter "yards" in late autumn and away from those winter quarters as soon as the first thaws begin are examples of cyclical annual movements. The white-tailed species is classified as non-migratory, of course, but there are examples in history (and in the present) where the miles traveled by a deer herd between its summering and wintering grounds can almost be described as migrations.

FOOD SOURCES

Ever-changing food sources constitute another major annual cycle that influences whitetail movement. Crops of favorite wild foods such as acorns, beechnuts and other forms of mast; fruits such as berries, wild plums, mayhaws, persimmons and mustang and muscadine grapes; mushrooms and other goodies; all can draw deer from great distances and concentrate them in small areas. It pays big dividends for hunters to familiarize themselves with the foods that whitetails prefer in a particular area and to scout for spots where those items are abundant. You can bet that the deer will be aware of food locations and of the food's degree of ripeness—and the hunter with the same knowledge will be miles ahead of the competition.

"The hunter with knowledge [of preferred foods] will be miles ahead of the competition ..."

Timing counts; many of these autumn deer groceries are available only for brief periods each season, and a grove or thicket where deer were abundant last week might hold only tracks and empty nut hulls today. It's not much trouble to compile a list on paper of the exact locations of various favored deer foods on your hunting grounds, with the dates of fruiting or mast-dropping periods noted from year to year. Such records, accumulated over several seasons, can offer invaluable predictions about where the deer can be found at different times in the future. Be aware, however, that these wild crops vary in abundance quite widely from year to year. Oaks seem to produce heavy acorn crops, for example, about every third year, and even this varies according to the amount and timing of rainfall.

Domestic apple and pear trees growing wild on old farms, in abandoned orchards or around

Bucks shed their antlers in places that offer security—the same places they seek out in severe weather or when pursued by predators.

vanished homesteads are examples of annual cyclical attractions. Agricultural crops, however, might or might not fit into this category. If always planted on the same schedule and never delayed by drought or other natural factors, field crops might be considered cyclical causes of whitetail movement. But such crops are often rotated, with certain fields lying fallow some years, and their attraction to deer is occasional rather than truly cyclical. They certainly do move deer around, however, and the farmer can usually give you a pretty good idea of when they ripen or otherwise become most attractive to deer.

PHOTOPERIOD AND THE RUT

Of all the cyclical events on the whitetail calendar, none is more reliable or dramatic than the rut. The reason is that the rut is actually timed and controlled by changes in the photoperiod, which is a big word for the changing length of the daylight period as the seasons advance.

The length of the daily period during which the retinas of a whitetail's eyes receive daylight influences the activity of the deer's pineal gland, which is buried at the base of its brain. The pineal gland, in turn, controls various hormone levels in the whitetail's bloodstream. One of these, the male hormone testosterone, controls the annual cycle of antler growth, velvet shedding, sperm production, dominance factors, courtship behaviors and antler drop in bucks. Actual mating is up to the female

Apples are an early-season delicacy for whitetails and can lure deer in areas where baiting is legal.

segment of the herd and is controlled by hormones that are ultimately physiological responses to changes in the photoperiod. The photoperiod, in turn, reflects the astronomical movements of the earth, sun and moon, and nothing can be more cyclical than that!

SHORT-TERM CYCLES

Most of the influences mentioned so far, being annual or seasonal, are responsible for long-term cycles in whitetail movements and are important to an overall understanding of how deer live their lives. They might not, however, be especially useful in the short-term planning of one's hunting time.

The lunar cycle is a prominent example of a short-term

cycle crucial to short-term planning. Every experienced hunter I've ever known has considered the moon an important element in hunting strategy. I've often said that the best time to go deer hunting is whenever you can, but if you have a choice, hunt during the dark of the moon.

As a matter more of curiosity than practical application, the lunar cycle has another effect on the whitetail lifestyle: the intervals between the recurring estrus periods of whitetail does average about 28 days, if not interrupted by conception. This fact suggests that rutting mini-peaks can occur about one month before and one month after the main rutting peak in a given hunting area. These mini-peaks, or false ruts, can create a disproportionate amount of deer movement. Bucks will be trailing, tending, fighting and engaging in a great deal of aggressive behavior—and it will all be over in about 48 hours. This activity is spotty, localized and might not be visible at all in some areas, but where it does occur it's often as exciting as the main rut itself.

INDIVIDUAL PATTERNS

There is much campfire chatter about the regular appearance of deer in the same place at somewhat regular intervals. The interval is estimated at anywhere from 24 hours to a week, but seems to occur most frequently in two- or three-day cycles. If there is really any pattern to a whitetail's movements, it will surely not be during the rut or when hunters are in the woods. Those influences would randomly disrupt any routine. Even in South Texas, where mature bucks might range over thousands of acres, they would not require a week, or even three days, to cover a regular beat around their home ranges. Bucks that I've been able to see repeatedly have most often appeared in the same place at about the same time at intervals of approximately one day.

Sometimes whitetails are eerily precise. I've watched the same buck cross a South Texas sendero (a raw dirt lane bulldozed through the brush) within 50 yards of the same place and within 30 minutes of the same hour every day for four days straight. So far, so good; the buck's personal pattern would seem to have been well established … but then it vanished, and I never saw that buck cross that particular sendero again!

Sometimes it works the other way around, and a buck is collected instead of spared because it broke its established pattern. One such buck was Bigfoot. We knew that this buck regularly crossed a sandy woods road, but for years we never saw the deer in the flesh. We knew it only by its

Keeping a logbook and referring back to it—while cross-referencing moon, weather and other information—can help you establish, and possibly even predict, general deer activity patterns.

> *"If there is really any pattern to a whitetail's movements, it will surely not be during the rut."*

track, which was so large and deep that it earned the animal its nickname. Fresh tracks appeared almost every morning, proving that it crossed the road during the night. In those days (the 1950s) we had no way of knowing the hour of its passing, but we hunted there at dawn almost every day, hoping to catch it coming home a little late. Had Bigfoot stuck to his schedule, he might have lived forever, but on a bitter-cold day after Christmas in 1959 the buck ambled across that road, for reasons known only to itself, at 10 a.m. and found a hunter shivering miserably beside a tiny fire of sticks. A. W. picked up his rifle, stepped across his fire to get a better view and shot Bigfoot dead in his oversized tracks. The buck's body matched his footprints; field-dressed, the deer was 40 percent heavier than the average mature buck in those parts and he was the heaviest buck we ever harvested on that ranch in more than 25 years. The buck was very old, however, and the rack proved disappointing for such a big-bodied animal.

Sometimes it's too easy. More than once I've noticed a buck in a certain place at a certain time

Bucks and does are rarely seen together except when a they've located a prime feeding area ... or when the rut is near.

of day and slipped in a day or two later, only to have the deer walk into my sights almost as though we had an appointment. A few such experiences can almost—but not quite—convince me that deer really do travel a circuit and appear on some sort of schedule.

⸻◦◦◦⸻

"Knowing where and when a buck has been sighted before is better than nothing ..."

⸻◦◦◦⸻

One year, I spent two full weeks trying to pattern the only true 7x7 typical 14-pointer I've ever seen in the wild. Had I succeeded, the deer might have been the highest-scoring buck I've taken. It was seen seven times during that fort-

night, not always by me but always within a quarter-mile stretch of road, and always between 11 a.m. and 1 p.m., with most sightings closer to 1 p.m. Naturally, we named him the "One O'Clock Buck." With a "book" as tight as that on a buck, you'd think he would have been easy to tag, but I could never do it. Knowing where and when a buck has been sighted before is better than nothing, but it's not necessarily enough to begin planning the taxidermy pose! It was not the first, nor will it be the last buck I ever meet that I cannot take, no matter how clever and persistent I might be.

Despite all that's written about patterning, I doubt that whitetails ever really fall into a pattern—at least not one lasting more than a few days. Certainly it's possible to see the same buck in the same soybean field every evening for a stretch in June, but any chance of seeing it there during deer season probably depends more heavily upon a seductive doe than on any pattern. Ah, if only it were as easy as the patterning proponents make it sound! We remember our successes and forget the much more numerous failures of patterning efforts, but a few good guesses don't prove the rule. (For more on patterning problems, see Charles Alsheimer's story, "Can You Really Pattern Deer?" in Chapter 2.)

"If only it were as easy as the patterning proponents make it sound!"

GETTING IN THE SWING

Despite my skepticism about working out a timetable on a certain buck's short-term movements, I don't mean to imply that there's no profit in plotting whitetail cycles. Every successful hunter does exactly that, one way or another. A successful hunter looks for information on the moon, considers past experience on the timing of the rut in the area, and keeps close track of the ripening schedules of favorite seasonal whitetail foods. All this is blended with a strong dash of intuition and a lot of patience and hard scouting, both in and out of season. The result is what seems to be an uncanny ability to forecast the whereabouts of buck deer at certain times. Do not allow such opportunities to pass unseized. Shoot the deer and then try to keep your face straight and accept the public admiration with suitable modesty and humility!

The cyclical comings and goings of a deer herd—that is, on annual, seasonal or lunar cycles—are regular but still arcane, more easily deduced than observed. These cycles affect all age groups and both sexes in the deer herd—perhaps to varying degrees. For example, an attractive agricultural field might produce mostly sightings of does, fawns and young bucks, but few mature males (at least until the rut begins). But a stroll across the field in early morning will probably reveal the big, deep tracks of unseen bucks—telling us that they're drawn to the field just like the does, only not during daylight.

WHEN CYCLES FAIL

Do the cycles ever change or fail completely? Well, the sun and the moon never fail to perform on schedule, and the seasons continue to roll with the calendar. Any almanac can tell us accurately which days of the year will be the longest and shortest, but

Midday, crossing a road! And you're on your way home for lunch.

worldwide weather patterns can and do change. Crops—both natural and agricultural—can vary in timing and abundance from year to year or even fail completely, altering the rhythms of whitetails in obvious ways.

Lean years are not necessarily unfavorable for hunters. In lush seasons with seemingly inexhaustible supplies of mast, the bucks have no reason to move around much before the rut starts and they tend to stick to heavy cover during the daylight hours. Bucks are present, but sightings from fixed stands will be fewer than normal. In years with no acorns, however, or when the winter oats or wheat fail, the deer must hustle day and night to find enough to eat and, therefore, can be seen more often. Likewise, in dry years in which the summer growth of annual ground cover is sparse, the animals are more visible simply because there's less undergrowth to hide them.

Likewise, radically unseasonable weather can alter deer behavior, perhaps driving the herd to its winter yards earlier than normal or forcing more movement to find enough to eat. Deer are quite sensitive to barometric changes (although we don't yet understand how they sense them in advance), so unusual autumn and winter storms can suppress movement or drive the animals to hole up in protected pockets. I locate these pockets in springtime by looking for shed antlers. Where the bucks take refuge from unusual or severe weather in autumn is also generally where they hang out during the normal hard weather of late winter—and that's where they tend to be when their antlers drop.

Fawn production varies from year to year and hinges on the quality of the habitat and the condition of the local deer herd.

These cycle-breaking events are always anomalies in weather patterns, temporary abnormalities that seldom persist for more than a few days and, excluding the exceptional drought, never for a whole year. They require, in other words, no long-term readjustments in your own thinking or hunting patterns and they do not invalidate all your past observations, notes and scouting.

UNDERSTANDING THE ELEMENTS

by John Wootters

A re weather conditions as all-important to whitetail movement as most writers claim? In a word, yes! Few modern hunters ever give much thought to the hardships to which deer and other wildlife are routinely subjected. Whitetails have no place to go to get out of the weather. Rain or shine, hot or cold, windy, foggy or icy, wild animals must simply endure it. Nor can whitetails put on or take off extra garments; they have no Gore-Tex, Thermax, Worsterlon or Thinsulate. But they do have a pretty weather-resistant all-natural coat ... and an amazing toughness, right down to the most delicate-looking fawns! Try going out there for a week in November or December wearing only one layer of buckskin (tanned hair-on), barefoot, bareheaded, no tent, no fire and no bedroll. Then come back and tell me whether weather matters!

The trouble is that we cannot know intuitively exactly how weather matters to a deer. All we can do is observe deer movement and correlate it with weather parameters and then try to deduce how whitetails respond to various sets of conditions and why.

Most of the serious deer hunters I've known have kept some kind of hunting journal or logbook in which they note day-to-day hunting experiences. Weather factors are among the most important information entered, together with numbers, sexes, sizes and actions of the deer seen. Over time these journals can accumulate a staggering body of data, but in a form from which it is difficult to extract meaningful correlations.

Tough to beat a frosty, still morning in the North. Cool weather often spurs feeding activity and simply makes it more tolerable for deer to travel.

DEER HUNTING DATABASE

I kept such journals for many years, eventually bogging down in the sheer mass of information. What I needed was a personal computer—except that such things hadn't been invented at the time I needed one.

Years later, my first computer was an Apple II+, the RAM capacity of which I expanded all the way to the maximum. There was no mouse, no hard drive, no cache, no modem, no fax card, no laser printer and no color monitor. Pretty primitive, you say? You bet! It still is. By the way, I still have it. The reason I keep the old Apple is because it can tell me how white-tailed deer react to weather, moon, rut and other factors in a way that nothing else in the world can.

I do not wish to convey the impression that I'm some sort

of computer whiz. I picked up the basic manual that came with the computer and slowly puzzled out the principles of programming and then, by trial and error, wrote a program to help me sort my deer-sighting data. My ignorance was so abysmal that I didn't know that a computer can't be made to do certain things, so I went ahead and did them. I'm confident that the result would be laughable to a real programmer. It's slow and strains the memory capacity of my creaky old computer, but it works. I just can't face the prospect of rewriting the program (even if I knew how) to run on my new super-hotshot IBM PC "clone," and I especially can't bear the thought of re-entering all the data.

—⌘—

"I've been keeping a careful record of deer sightings on our ranch for 15 consecutive seasons ..."

—⌘—

You see, I've been keeping a careful record of deer sightings on our ranch for 15 consecutive seasons, along with daily recordings of nine different weather and environmental parameters. As this is written, a total of 8,842 deer have been seen in 15 years—2,611 bucks and 6,231 does. To enter those sightings in a new program would amount to almost 180,000 keystrokes! So I just keep the old Apple and put up with its leisurely operational speed.

Eyeballing those 8,800 deer required the expenditure of 809.5 hunter-days, including all or parts of 319 actual calendar days, during 15 hunting seasons. That comes out to almost 11 deer sighted per hunter-day, of which 3.2 have had antlers. Some interesting statistics, and meaningful trends—as in the observed buck-to-doe ratio—extending over several years can be identified and analyzed. The sex ratio has ranged from a low of one buck for every 4.3 does to a high of a one buck to 1.4 does, and has averaged 1:2.8. For the two most recent years the ratio has been 1:1.4 and 1:1.6, indicating that we've been doing something right management-wise.

DUPLICATE SIGHTINGS

Interestingly, although my records reveal that we average well more than 500 whitetail sightings per season, the best estimates (from helicopter surveys and other census methods) put the actual total deer population of the property at somewhere between 100 and 200 adult animals. That means we average seeing each individual deer at least three times during the hunting season and maybe as many as five times.

My guess is that we never see certain animals at all, and that we see others many times. I'll also guess that the bucks show up maybe 1.5 times per season each, on average, and the does six or seven times. However, it really doesn't matter whether my guesses are correct; as long as I use the same methods of data collection and analysis from year to year, the trends extracted from this mass of sightings are still valid.

Likewise, the data concerning conditions are also valid. Each of those 8,842 sightings is tied to all of the following parameters: day, week and month of the season; wind direction and velocity; sky conditions, including precipitation; barometric status and movement; phase of the moon; and temperature. I recorded all these parameters twice for each day on which hunting took place, once in the morning and once in the afternoon. The only significant weather factor that I did not record was the relative humidity, which I left out for two reasons. One—I didn't have an accurate and reliable instrument for recording humidity. Two—humidity did not at the time seem to be a significant factor in whitetail movement. I now regret this omission and believe that the humidity data might have been illuminating, but it's too late

A cool day in Texas might be warm for a Wisconsin whitetail. It's all relative. And cooler than normal means more movement than normal.

There's no doubt about it—good records are important in deer hunting! A hunting journal is a valuable piece of equipment for veteran whitetail hunters.

now; there are already 15 years and more than 800 hunter-days of data recorded without it.

There are other probable deficiencies in the design of this project. In hindsight, it would have been valuable to know during what hour of the morning or afternoon each deer was seen, but the burden of recording sightings and parameters was already becoming unwieldy and I drew the line there. For another, the exact barometer readings might have helped, but the system I used—which simply notes whether the barometer is rising, falling or standing steady—is adequate.

The database is "uniquely authoritative as to how whitetail movement is altered by environmental conditions ..."

For lack of a better name, the whole effort is called the Los Cuernos Database. "Los Cuernos" is Spanish for "the antlers" and is the name of the ranch on which all this work has been carried out. The Los Cuernos Database is, I'm told, unique. It holds nearly 9,000 individual deer sightings made over 15 consecutive open seasons on the same property, with every sighting tied to the conditions existing during each hunting day. I also consider it uniquely authoritative as to how whitetail movement is altered by environmental conditions on Los Cuernos Ranch. Elsewhere, whitetails will very likely exhibit somewhat different responses, although probably only in degree. Furthermore, I believe that this program yields results that can be reliably extrapolated to other lati-

tudes, longitudes and climates, although not without a little speculation and interpretation.

DATA OUTPUT

One of the key features of my home-written software program is that it answers each question asked of it in two ways. For example, if I ask it how many bucks I've seen on days following a full moon, it gives the answer as a raw number and as a percentage of all the bucks in the database. It also tells how many of the days on which those sightings were made were in full moon periods and, again, what percentage of all the days in the database were full moon days. For a more concrete example, if it shows that only 3 percent of all the bucks in the database were seen on days following full moon nights, that number merely implies a conclusion. But when the program then indicates that only 3 percent of all the observed bucks appeared under conditions that occurred during a full 21 percent of all the days hunted, that draws its own conclusion in my mind, which is that buck hunting is lousy on days after bright nights.

WIND DIRECTION

My research has revealed that whitetails could care less about wind direction. However, they do respond strongly to certain barometric conditions. The tricky part is that a northwest wind in this part of the continent is usually associated with a rapidly rising barometer and the onset of a weather front. The barometric movement affects the deer, not the wind direction.

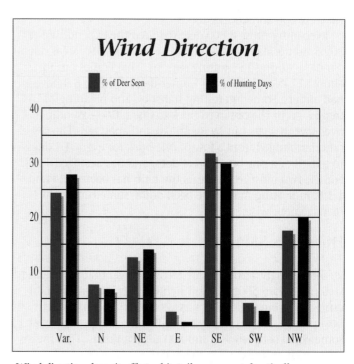

Wind direction doesn't affect whitetail movement drastically.

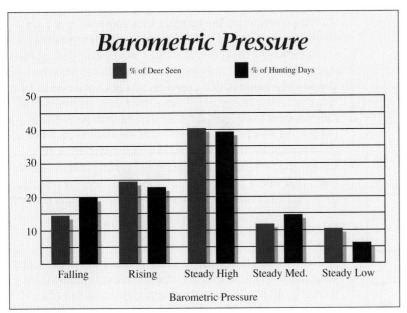

Whitetails move more with a moving barometer, especially a rising one.

BAROMETER

Deer themselves make a pretty good barometer. Back in the late 1930s and '40s I was hunting out of the old Fonville camp. The most significant topographic feature of the area was Big Sandy Creek. Big Sandy snakes for miles across the coastal prairie through picturesque live oaks draped with Spanish moss, and along its banks grows a large and very dense yaupon thicket. Almost impenetrable by hunters, this thicket is the best available wildlife shelter for miles around.

We had no barometer in camp, nor did we need one. Whenever we observed that most deer were moving into the thicket, we knew that a weather front was on the way. When the whitetails began to move out of the thicket a day or two later, the storm was past and better weather was coming. Not only were the deer infallible, but they were also very early indicators of weather to come. Their behavior foretold the arrival of atmospheric high- and low-pressure areas a full 24 hours before the U.S. Weather Bureau radio broadcasts could do so.

The Los Cuernos Database says that whitetails prefer a moving barometer to a steady one and that they move about more when it's rising than when it's falling. If the barometer is neither rising nor falling, however, they show a slight preference for a high steady reading over a low steady one.

SKY CONDITIONS

I'll plead "not guilty" to any charge of loading my database to prove my own pet theories. I certainly had my share of theories about how deer respond to weather and the moon, but the Los Cuernos Database has left a couple of them in shambles!

A long-time favorite theory of mine was that whitetails prefer clear weather and that deer movement would vary inversely with the percentage of the sky covered by clouds. This was not merely an opinion but almost an article of faith with me. If I were a gambling man, I'd have bet a substantial chunk of change that the computer would prove that the less cloudy the sky, the greater the number of deer sighted. Not by the hair of my chinny-chin-chin! I was stunned to find out that there's absolutely no statistically significant correlation between sky conditions and whitetail movement ... or at least not one that cannot more logically be explained by other factors, such as barometer and/or wind force. This and the animals' abovementioned indifference to wind direction have been the biggest surprises yet squeezed out of the database by the old Apple.

TEMPERATURE

The database dug up some other unexpected results as well. One is about temperature. I imagine that all hunters, wherever they hunt, would agree with the assumption that hot weather suppresses deer movement. My computer agrees with that hypothesis, but with a surprising twist. Los Cuernos Ranch is located very near the Tex-Mex border and is distinctly subtropical in climate. The deer there are used to warm weather, even during hunting season. Even so, every experienced South Texas hunter knows that deer move better on crisp, cool mornings and that hot afternoons, although not uncommon, are usually pretty slow. I was con-

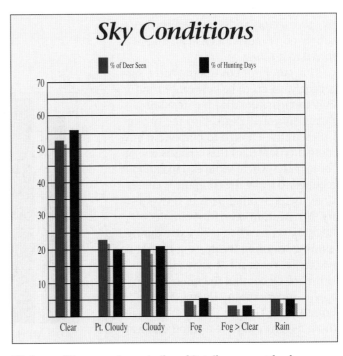

All sky conditions experience similar whitetail movement levels.

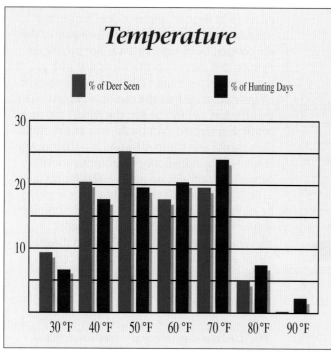

There is a comfort range in which whitetail movement is normal. Too hot or cold, movement drops.

fident that the computer would agree that the higher the temperature, the less deer activity, and vice versa.

It did no such thing! The data proved that there is a certain critical temperature above which whitetail activity tends almost to stop and below which movement remains normal. In other words, there is no more movement when the mercury is in the 40s than when it is in the 50s. A more accurate picture reveals a sort of cutoff point on the thermometer, below which deer activity is controlled by other factors and above which they simply don't move much at all unless forced to do so.

That cutoff for Los Cuernos deer, surprisingly, seems to be between 60 and 70°F (temperature data is entered in increments of 10 degrees, so the system isn't sensitive enough to pinpoint it any more precisely than that). This is one of those places where some extrapolation is required to make the computer's conclusions useful in other parts of the country. A Wisconsin deer, for example, might never have felt a 70°F day during hunting season in its life, so it cannot be set to click on or off at such a level. However, I'll bet that the same pattern applies in Wisconsin, Alberta, New Brunswick or Georgia. The deer herds in those regions will have a cutoff temperature of their own that matches the climate where they live. Maybe a Michigan

deer lies down when the mercury rises above 40°F, or a Virginia deer might start traveling when the temperature slips below 50°F. Whatever the exact local cutoff point, observation should reveal one once we know what to look for. The key revelation is that deer activity does not respond to rising or falling temperature like a chandelier responds to a dimmer switch—in graduated increments. It's more like a normal light switch—either on or off, depending on whether the temperature is above or below a fairly narrow range. It should also be repeated that below the cutoff point, whatever point that might prove to be for your local deer, weather factors other than temperature tend to control whitetail activity.

WIND VELOCITY

The pattern of response to wind force is somewhat similar. Most hunters believe that deer movement is suppressed by strong, gusty winds. Such winds obviously make all of a whitetail's early warning systems—eyes, ears and nose—less reliable. Therefore, the logic would seem to suggest the harder the wind, the less whitetail movement.

Like the temperature effect, this is correct—sort of. The actual situation is that, as in the temperature gradient, there is a cutoff point. When wind velocity is above this point, movement is inhibited. Below the critical velocity, movement seems to proceed fairly normally, again being more affected by other factors. According to my database, that cutoff point on Los Cuernos is between 20 and 25 miles per hour (wind velocities are entered into the database in 5 mph increments). I'll bet there's a similar cutoff velocity where you hunt as well but that it is not necessarily the same as ours. It is probably just above the highest wind speed that's

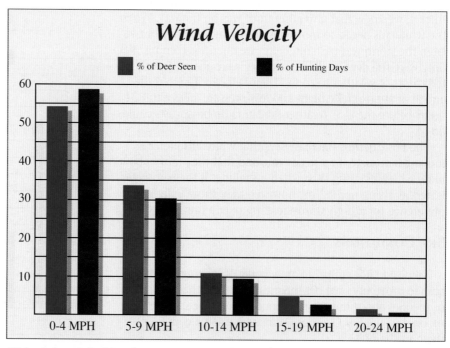

High winds curtail whitetail movement.

─୦∕୦∕୦─

"Nothing cancels barometric pressure as an influence on deer movement, and nothing overcomes the imperative of an active rut. I believe the phase of the moon ranks right up there as an important predictor of movement and that temperature is important when it gets to the critical cutoff point."

─୦∕୦∕୦─

common during hunting season. If you live on the prairies of Alberta or Saskatchewan, the wind force that puts the deer down might be upwards of 30 mph. If you hunt in quiet country, it could be lower than ours. In any case, I'd expect that the most meticulous record-keeping possible cannot prove that your deer move about any more freely when the wind is calm than they do when it's blowing 10 or 12 mph, contrary to widespread popular belief.

IN CONCLUSION

Not one of these factors exercises absolute control of whitetail movement. All factors must be evaluated in order to estimate the probabilities of deer activity during any given period. The temperature might cancel out the wind velocity, or the moon might negate the influence of sky conditions. All must be considered as a whole.

However, based on many years of generating and studying the Los Cuernos Database, I'll offer my opinion that nothing cancels barometric pressure as an influence on deer movement, and nothing overcomes the imperative of an active rut. I believe the phase of the moon ranks right up there as an important predictor of movement and that temperature is important when it gets to the critical cutoff point.

These, at least, are the things those 8,842 deer in the Los Cuernos Database are whispering in my ear. And do they inform me as to the best time to go deer hunting? Sure! Whenever I can get away!

RUT CRAZED

by John Wootters

It's not difficult to find signs that the rut is on. What is difficult is predicting where a buck will be at any given time during his chase of does.

The rut—the breeding season—is the one and only infallible movement maker for white-tailed deer. When the rut is on, nothing will suppress whitetail movement, especially the male segment of the herd. A rutting buck will move more or less incessantly, day and night, in any kind of weather, regardless of the phase of the moon. A rutting buck is even prepared to hustle hot does in the face of fairly heavy hunting pressure, something that normally causes bucks to vanish quicker than a puff of smoke in a hurricane. Excessive human disturbance in the woods can switch some rutting activity to nighttime (when a lot of it happens anyway), but can never stop it completely.

A DIFFERENT ANIMAL

Senior bucks fall completely out of character at this time of year. I've had one literally stalk all around my blind at the peak of the rut, knowing full well that I was in it and what I was. I've even seen a buck so preoccupied with trailing a hot doe, nose to the ground, that it actually ran bang into the fender of my truck. Many bucks seem almost suicidal when the rut gets really cranked up.

Passing along one's genetic heritage is the supreme imperative of all living creatures. Suddenly, their existence centers on performing the only action that biologically justifies their lives. In their scheme of things, servicing as many estrus does as possible and surviving are of equal importance. Accordingly, some do not survive the exertions and risks of the rut, falling to stress, wounds

Never is a whitetail buck more attainable, and easier to get extremely close to, than during the rut. You can kill a good buck at other times during the season, but this is the time when even the oldest bucks are vulnerable.

from other bucks and predators (human and otherwise). Hunting authors have known for 100 years that if an old buck is ever to make a fatal mistake, it will be during the rut. I've said repeatedly in print that the highest of the whitetail hunting arts might simply be placing and preparing oneself to take advantage of a rutting buck's mistakes.

THE PHASES OF THE RUT

One of the reasons for the frenetic quality of the rut is that the bucks don't have much time to fulfill this annual rite. The strenuous, highly conspicuous activity that we humans call "the rut" is actually only the peak period of the rut, a two- to three-week time when there are more does in estrus simultaneously than at any other time. Depending upon your choice of indicators, it might be said that the whole rut lasts from the time the first buck polishes the velvet from its antlers in autumn until the last one sheds its antlers in wintertime, a period of about five months. Anytime a buck has hard antlers, it's able and more than willing to impregnate a doe. During this time its testicles will be descended and manufacturing sperm, its tarsal (hock) glands will be visibly active and its

neck will be swollen.

The male, however, is not the one that makes it all happen. The female controls that. For does, the rut probably lasts only a few hours. As soon as, or even a little before, the doe enters its estrus (heat) period, it will doubtless acquire masculine companionship, and as soon as the doe conceives, it cycles out of estrus for that year. Should a doe fail to conceive for some reason, the estrus period will end about 26

"[The] activity that we humans call 'the rut' is actually only the peak period ..."

hours after it began, and the deer will enter another one 28 days later. In a single season, a doe can theoretically have as many as four of these cycles, but it's almost impossible for this ever to actually happen in the wild. For most does in

29

The rut is a good time to get aggressive. Whether you incorporate scents, calls, rattling devices or decoys in your approach, it's time to try pulling bucks to your stand.

hierarchy, are prowling, constantly keeping an eye out—and a nose curled in the so-called Flehmen gesture—for a doe that might be nearing its first estrus cycle. Any doe that a buck meets in its daily rounds is "tested." Approaching the doe in a characteristic posture with head lowered and neck extended, the buck's chin is raised, its antlers are rocked backward making them less menacing, and its ears are laid back. In this position, the buck walks or trots straight at the object of its affection. If the doe does not flee but simply stands there with her tail held horizontal and to one side, the buck has just gotten lucky. The buck simply walks up and mounts the doe. Quite a lot of breeding takes place in this manner, contrary to much of the deer hunting literature.

BATTLE OF THE SEXES

On the other hand, if the doe is not receptive, it flees the advancing buck, which usually chases the doe for a few yards. If the doe really isn't ready, the buck abandons the chase quickly and looks around for another. If the doe is just being coy, however, the buck will detect that fact by scent and by Flehmen (we really don't know exactly what information is transferred via the Flehmen procedure, but males of all cloven-hoofed mammals on earth practice it) and will try to run the doe down.

A buck will consciously try to herd a fleeing doe into the open where she has fewer shrubs and trees around which to dodge, and the buck will sometimes place himself between the doe and the nearest heavy cover and "work" the doe, exactly like a cutting horse works a calf, to prevent the doe from breaking past and reaching the cover. I've also seen bucks use a corner in a fence to hem up a reluctant doe.

Once the doe yields to his advances, the buck will tend the doe, remaining close as long as the doe's estrus period lasts. They might copulate repeatedly, but, except for that activity, nothing that my wife would call a "relationship" is to be seen. The buck is, however, deeply in love, and follows the doe—usually at a little distance—wherever it might go, rarely taking his eyes off the doe. If another buck tries to approach the happy couple, the buck in charge will try to drive it away—or kill it, if it comes to combat! Most serious buck fights occur when a hot doe leads a current lover into the range of another dominant buck.

reasonably well-balanced herds, the first estrus period is also the last.

DEFINING THE RUT

A few does, usually the older ones, come into estrus a month or so before the majority of their sisters, and a few come in for the first time, or recycle, a month or so later. This makes a graph of rutting activity assume, roughly, the shape of a bell curve, representing about a three-month period, with most of the activity concentrated in the middle month of the three.

Latitude can shift the rut cycle by a full 60 days. Some herds in the north begin in September and are about wound down by the end of November, whereas some southern herds get going in November, peak in December, and might still be swinging by the end of January. However, whatever the latitude, the sequence and schedule of events remains the same.

As mentioned in "Living with Deer," the rut is timed and triggered by the photoperiod. As the days of autumn grow shorter, the daily length of sunlight eventually arrives at the correct duration to trigger the hormonal responses of the deer. The bucks, having already established a dominance

As soon as the doe cycles out of estrus, the boyfriend splits and begins prospecting for a new hot doe. As the season progresses toward the peak of the rut, the bucks become more and more excited and active and roam almost continuously, testing every doe they encounter.

"Bucks ... roam almost continuously, testing every doe they encounter."

Obvious Signs

In the meantime, bucks are busy making rubs and scrapes to advertise their proprietorship of a breeding area and their availability for stud service. Scrapes are an important, but still somewhat mysterious, element in the whole complex of rutting behavior. A dominant buck makes a scrape (or freshens one made by another buck) by pawing the ground and urinating in the disturbed earth, usually in such a position that the urine runs down over the buck's tarsal glands as they are rubbed together. Presumably, this deposits the buck's own distinctive scent in the scrape. Just as important as the actual scratching of the earth with his front hooves is the buck's treatment of a twig or branch that invariably overhangs the scrape (see photo on page 28). The buck meshes this in his antlers and whips it about, chews and licks it and sometimes snaps it off so that it falls into the scrape. A whitetail buck can perform this act with his antlers more deftly than you could do with both hands!

The buck will probably make several scrapes close together in sequence, sometimes defecating as well as urinating in them, occasionally even ejaculating in one. The meaning of much of this behavior remains, frankly, obscure, and even what we think we know about it might be wrong. But we know that this occurs at least occasionally: A doe needs a buck during the relatively brief estrus. And if a buck fails to find the doe, the doe will go looking for a buck. During this search, the doe is attracted to fresh scrapes by scent and visits them, one by one. Dominant bucks spend a good deal of time in the vicinity of their central (or "hub," or "core") scrapes, so the doe may find a date at the scrape itself.

If the proprietor is absent, our doe will deposit her own urinary calling card in or near the scrape and wander off, secure in the certainty that the buck will be by shortly.

And he will, too, scent trailing the doe like a hound, nose to the ground. As they trail, bucks grunt like pigs, apparently out of sheer excitement, every few seconds. They also grunt sometimes when tending a hot doe.

Eventually, the buck will follow the trail to the doe, and the liaison is consummated, providing the doe hasn't picked up another boyfriend since visiting the scrape. In that case, if the two bucks are fairly well matched in body and antler, they declare war. These particular buck fights are not mere sparring matches but serious efforts to destroy the opponent. Where the bucks are powerful enough, they might literally fight to the death of one or both. In one recent season, I found two bucks dead of antler wounds—one in Michigan and the other in southern Texas—and my famous, gentle-but-free-ranging friend, Bucky, a savage fighter, might have met his end in that way.

Obviously, all these rut related activities—testing does, tending does, chasing does, trailing does, making rubs and scrapes, fighting other bucks—distract from a buck's time to do the other important activities such as eating and evading hunters. They also promote an immense amount of deer activity that does not occur during other seasons. How can we hunters take advantage of all this ruckus?

Rut Hunting Tactics

To begin with, we must realize that rutting is a 24-hour-a-day activity, regardless of weather, moon or anything else.

Scents define the rut. Here a buck urinates over his tarsal glands while rubbing them together, depositing the result into a scrape.

31

That means we must spend every possible minute in the woods at this time of year. In stand hunting, I like to sit where I can see the greatest possible sweep of habitat, on the theory that the more country I can cover, the better chance I have of spotting the buck that I want, even if I have to leave my stand and try to go to him.

"You cannot rattle a buck
away from a hot doe!"

Needless to say, antler rattling and aggressive grunting are both sounds associated with the rut, but they must be employed judiciously. Loud, fierce antler rattling, simulating a really serious fight, is most effective during the week or so just before the peak of the rut. Bucks will come to rattling during the peak itself, but only if they do not happen to be in the company of a hot doe. And during the rut's peak,

most dominant bucks are with one doe or another most of the time.

You can record this and say I wrote it: You cannot rattle a buck away from a hot doe! You will do well to make a buck take a few steps from the doe's side or stick his head out of a thicket, and that might be enough, but a buck will never actually leave a doe for your fake fight. During the "retirement" fortnight just after the peak of the rut, rattling or aggressive grunting might actually drive a big buck away.

I also like to still-hunt during the rut because the bucks are on the move, less alert for danger and more likely to let me get close. I think that the rut is the best time to use a deer decoy and the worst time to bait deer—where that's legal—unless you can bait up a hot doe.

PREDICTING THE RUT

To make the most of hunting opportunities associated with the rut, we need to know when it will happen. The rut's timing—or at least our perception of that timing—varies slightly from year to year, but usually by no more than a few days. I have seen a whitetail herd violate that statement only two years out of 50. In one of those seasons we had every

In many cases, firearms seasons overlap the rut or occur very close to this period. If the deer aren't intensively pressured, gun hunters can also notice the increase in buck sightings.

indication of a peaking rut almost a month before the customary starting time! It was an exceptionally good year and the herd was in superior body condition, and that might explain the early peak. If not, I'm at a loss. In most years, the easiest way to know when the rut will peak is to know when it peaked last year and other recent years.

Where there is a high ratio of bucks to does, I've often noticed a conspicuous build-up of fresh rubs in the woods just before the peak of the rut. Then, as the rut climaxes, there might be a virtual explosion of new rubs almost overnight. Buck rubs signal where buck movement will occur, usually marking routes or corridors regularly used by bucks. I have taken several fine bucks over the years by staking out fresh rub lines. Rubs are often concentrated where two such routes intersect. In every part of the country, whitetails prefer one or two sapling species over all others for rubbing, and these usually have smooth bark and resinous sap—pines, cedars, hemlocks and the like. Bucks often return to the same exact places year after year to rub and scrape. If a sapling survives the early years of rubbing, the scars will probably be visible for the life of the tree. In certain soil types old scrapes, too, are quite persistent.

ANOMALIES IN THE RUT

You know what they say about the course of true love, and the whitetail version, the rut, sometimes runs anything but smoothly. In some years the rutting peak is a concentrated pulse of activity, as described earlier in this chapter, lasting about two to three weeks. Hunters I know have come to regard this as the "normal" pattern. In other years the pattern is entirely different; a long, drawn-out, stop-and-start sort of rut that seems never to peak at all. In a few other seasons the impression is that there simply was no rut at all. Yet there is always a fresh crop of fawns the following spring to show how wrong outsiders' impressions can be.

These differing courses of the rut might result from different weather patterns, varying demographics within the herd or perhaps even different patterns of hunting pressure. And I believe that the drawn-out, off-and-on rut is the most common on my hunting grounds. In any case, you should know that these variations do occur and be prepared to adapt to them. How? Well, of this I'm sure: always assume that the rut is in progress whenever the date is inside the traditional time boundaries for your area, even when you've actually seen little or no sign of it.

During a couple of those slow-rut or late-rut seasons I've let half or more of the peak slip by me because I was too pig-headed to believe that it could be in progress without my knowing it. And the rut is much too important to miss even

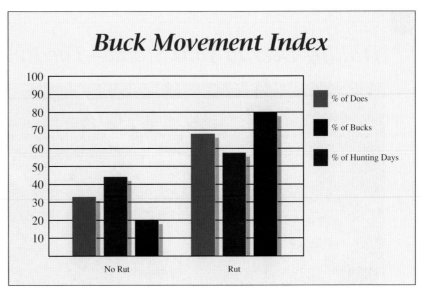

This graph shows that 80% of the Los Cuernos bucks were seen during the rut, although only 57% of the hunting days occurred then. Note that only 20% of the bucks were seen when the rut was not in progress, but 43% of the hunting days occurred on those non-rutting days. The effect on doe sightings follows the same pattern but is not quite so pronounced.

one day of it!

Another of my home-written software programs is designed to calculate and picture rutting activity graphically. I call the result the Buck Movement Index and have instructed the computer to draw a bar chart of buck activity over the whole season, day by day. I include on this page a chart from Los Cuernos in recent years to illustrate the different patterns that the rut can take. Technically, the entire Texas open hunting season is within the broadest definition of the whitetail breeding season, so what is shown in this chart is actually the peak of the rut.

Another sign of a rut-in-progress, besides a proliferation of rubs and scrapes, is a noticeable increase in the number of solitary does and fawns in the woods, separated by jealous bucks and the doe's instinctive unwillingness to allow a male fawn to follow her as she enters estrus. Solitary bucks are another sign, and bucks running together signal that the rut is not yet serious. The tarsal glands of adult does turn black and tarry as they approach estrus. Obviously, rut-related activities on the part of the bucks—trailing, chasing and tending does and serious fighting among themselves—don't happen except during the rut. As mentioned, some years these signs are more subtle than others, but they're never entirely absent during the major portion of the mating season.

I have called the rut the major movement maker among whitetails, and that's true. In fact, perhaps the very best sign that the rut is going is the sudden drastic increase in sightings of moving deer, especially bucks.

Trailing Deer to Your Stand—The Rut

Wind

Drag Wick

Hang Wick

B

C3

C2

C1

A1

Apply Scent

20 Yards

A2

30 to 40 Yards

Apply More Scent

Bedding Area

Park

Hunter's Path

Stand Placement

Feeding Area

*I*n the accompanying illustration, we have attempted to lay out a realistic deer-hunting situation. As is most often the case, the deer have a number of trails that they might choose to travel—or they might not keep to the trails at all. As a result, many hunters attempt to lure the deer to them with scent as the rut approaches.

Making a scent trail does not require any great level of expertise. It isn't fancy. But it does require that you consider things like wind direction and where the deer are likely to cross *your* trail. And it does add to the realism of your setup compared to dumping a few drops of scent on the leaves around your stand.

Some hunters put scent on their boots as soon as they start walking from the truck. But if your stand is more than a few hundred yards away, you're generally better off getting closer before you apply any scent. In fact, as indicated in the diagram, many hunters choose to apply the scent first at a point within range of the stand (point A1). Since you might spill a bit of scent on the ground, you want this concentration to be in a possible target area. In addition, a buck following the scent of a hot doe might expect the scent concentration to get stronger as he trails. Thus, more scent should be within range of your stand than out at the perimeter of the scent trail.

Wearing knee-high rubber boots and latex gloves, apply the scent to a wick attached to a short (three-foot) length of string (see sketch illustrating point A1). Then take a circuitous route, attempting to cut deer trails out of range of your stand location (see dotted line and sketch illustrating point B). Loop back toward your stand and re-apply some scent as you get just within shooting range (point A2). Continue on out front of your stand and soak two additional wicks, hanging them from tree branches approximately four to five feet off the ground so that the wind will hit them. These wicks should be well within range of your stand (points C1 and C2). Finally, take the string and wick from around your boot and hang it in the same manner in front of your stand (point C3).

You'll note that the scent is not applied directly to the boots or tracked up to the tree your stand is in. You don't want the buck walking to the base of your tree and wondering whether that's supposed to be a hot doe up in the treestand. You want him in range but with his attention away from you. In fact, you should put the scent bottle and latex gloves in a zip-lock bag after you've finished hanging the last wick.

Like any other whitetail hunting technique, scent trails have their good and bad moments. But they work often enough that many deer hunters think it's worth the extra walk before climbing up into the treestand—especially as the rut approaches.

—Gregg Gutschow

Chapter 2

GOING TO WORK

nless you have the dollars and plenty of time to get away to hunt with a whitetail outfitter, you'll measure your whitetail success by the price you pay in scouting.

Yes, you've heard it all before. You've been preached to enough about this scouting stuff. And you'll do it. A couple weeks before the season you'll check out your old stand sites, look for fresh sign, maybe even glass a couple of fields one night after work. You're scouting all right. But are you really getting anywhere?

The stories that comprise this chapter will demonstrate that your scouting ought to be much more than you've ever thought it to be. You'll find that you can learn things about deer year-round that will help you come hunting season. That's right. There is value in winter forays to the deer woods, springtime shed antler hunting, summer field watching. And during it all, there are other landowners to talk to and more properties to check out.

Sound like work? Well, it shouldn't feel that way even though you might decide to start devoting more hours to learning all you can about whitetails. Our bet is that you'll find that learning more about the deer you're hunting can be just as fun as the actual hunting season.

Another bet: If you take heed of some of the information in these next four stories, you'll undoubtedly climb into your stand on opening day a much more confident deer hunter. And that's a big step toward success …

A Plan that Pays

by Gene and Barry Wensel

Better deer hunting means paying close attention to deer sign and habitat throughout the seasons—both when the season's open and when it isn't.

Every serious hunting effort needs a plan. Techniques might vary a little nationally, but the basic idea in whitetail hunting is to allow or encourage deer movement past the ambush spot of a waiting hunter. Because of the very nature of a mature whitetail buck, we're usually much better off letting him come to us rather than the other way around.

Over the years, hunters have been bombarded with schemes, apparatus and revolutionary "new" techniques. There are several reasons for this. First, most hunters have a hunger for new information. Second, some hunters are always on the lookout for an easier way.

NO MAGIC FORMULA

A so-called "magic formula" doesn't exist. Tagging a good buck is the reward for lots of time and effort. It's unfortunate that so many hunters try to take shortcuts these days when the satisfaction as well as rewards of a hunt lie in direct proportion to the expression of the physical act itself. Whatever happened to going out to the "back 40" for a simple hunt? You and the game. One on one. Predator versus prey. Satisfaction need not lie in just the hunt nor just the kill but in the sum total of the outdoor experience.

Laziness is an erosion of man's nature. Consider the analogy of inheriting a fortune versus building your own wealth. Sure, it'd be nice to inherit a pile of money without the work or headaches. But the fact remains, if it's lost, it's lost forever. On the other hand, a self-motivated individual who uses his own brain to build wealth not only has the satisfaction in knowing he's done it himself, but he's also acquired the knowledge to do it all over again. Loss of an entire fortune doesn't erase the ability to gain it all back.

The same applies to hunting trophy bucks. You can shoot a trophy buck or you can hunt and shoot him. How an

It doesn't get much better than this. The hunter who dedicates the time to keep tabs on a buck like this deserves to tag him.

animal is taken often reflects on a hunter's integrity and character.

Knowledge gained through experience builds personal wealth in hunting values. Not only do you have the satisfaction gained through effort, but you've more than likely learned something, too. If you go on a guided hunt, try to learn from your guide. Acquire knowledge that you might be able to adapt elsewhere.

About half of the hunting population wants and expects the "experts" to tell them that in order to shoot big bucks one has to have a formula. They want to hear that they should be wearing a certain type of boot with the toes pointed north. They want to be told the "big secret." If they don't hear it, they feel shortchanged, rejected and downright cheated. Fact is, there is no big secret. Success comes from application of accumulated knowledge spent hunting in a good area.

Knowledge is all but worthless without application. With

"Confidence leads to patience.
And patience leads to success."

wisdom comes the power of good judgment and the ability to follow a sound course of action based on experience as well as understanding. Scouting accumulates woods knowledge. We know people who don't start scouting until a few days before season opens. A lot more try to scout only while they're hunting. Both attitudes are wrong when you're interested in developing full personal potential. Because scouting is essentially learning through observation, we never stop. Scouting leads to understanding. Understanding leads to

Seeing the velvet come off, knowing he's there ... it all leads to confidence.

Additional pressure comes from family responsibilities that have often been ignored during the season. Fall projects have been put on the back burner. What comes next? Holidays. Deer are in winter yarding areas and shouldn't be disturbed, you say. Then comes spring, with pregnant does, fishing season, turkey hunting and gardening. June brings graduations, weddings and yard work. July and August? Too damn hot. Vacation. Bugs. Too much vegetation to see well. What's left? The usual answer: Scout during fall while hunting or maybe go up to camp a couple days early.

"Scouting year-round teaches us what deer do under various circumstances."

This is one of the most common mistakes hunters make. Why do ball players have spring training? They don't loosen up or practice their skills during the first few games of ball season and hope to be a winning team. The time to refine techniques is before season, so they'll be at their peak for the very first game. Each game afterward can be considered more of a learning experience. Get all your homework done. Goals should be set, plans made, schedules worked out, new areas scouted and most treestands up well before you hunt.

Some hunters tell us they don't scout in winter because information gained might not be relevant to deer activity during the season. Summer scouting gives patterns determined mostly

confidence. Confidence leads to patience. And patience leads to success.

Scouting might be better termed "on-the-job training." We are students of white-tailed deer. Practical application in the field, combined with studying and reading, forms true potential. Mix a burning desire to learn, a bit of common sense and time. These ingredients can't help but create a good deer hunter.

EXCUSES, EXCUSES

Hunters come up with dozens of reasons not to scout. Right after the season it's time to give the deer a rest.

by agricultural crops not necessarily available in fall. Fine ... to a point. But scouting year-round teaches us what deer do under various circumstances and wind conditions. It gives us the opportunity to predict behavior. Scouting prepares us both mentally and physically. Exercise of lungs and muscles gets us in better shape. Fresh air feeds brain cells and drains stress. Time in the outdoors during decent weather is always quality time.

On the other hand, don't use scouting as an "excuse," either. We all know "experts" who use the all-encompassing activity "scouting" as the primary reason for their success. They love to convince everyone who listens that they outsmarted their bucks by thorough scouting, exceptional detective work and a high degree of remarkable hunting skills. If the truth were known, the man simply has a great place to hunt and the time and money to do so. We're not saying that woodsmanship is not important. We're constantly looking for new places to hunt. We periodically spot-check and routinely monitor those areas that we're already familiar with. The point is this: once we learn an area, not much changes. Sure, there are exceptions. If someone builds a house in your favorite woodlot or if a pack of free-roaming dogs or a mountain lion moves into the area, deer movement will surely be affected. But barring anything beyond routine changes in immediate environment, a hunter should be able to go back years later and effectively hunt an area with minimal scouting.

LEARNING THE LAND

A few seasons back we hunted a farm that we hadn't set foot on in four years. We didn't get a chance to scout it. Yet we knew the place like the back of our hands, from previous years of scouting and hunting there. We went in "cold." We did maybe 15 minutes of "scouting," if you want to call it that. The farmer had rotated his crops and put in one small access road during the four years that we were absent. Other than that, not much had changed. Directional deer movement sign was about like we remembered it.

We quietly erected one treestand that afternoon, backed off and, the very next afternoon, took a buck that scored 156 Boone and Crockett Club points. We hunt lots of places a long distance from our homes. We simply don't have time to be scouting year-round maybe 500 miles away. Nor do we have to. We already know the areas inside and out.

Off-season scouting is a great way to gain new access, learn about deer habits and get in shape. But you're not going to learn much from any given buck or "deer area" in June that will help you kill that same buck come next November. About the only variable that stays the same from June until November is terrain. Everything else, including the deer themselves, is different.

Overkill on "in-season" scouting only disturbs deer or often ends up defeating our purpose. Scout to learn an area and gain access. Find feeding and bedding areas and security cover. Once you've figured out deer movement, monitor the area, set your stand up accordingly, slip in and hunt undisturbed deer. You'll be far better off than trying to scout full time. Scout year-round, but scout right.

When we first moved to Montana, we spent the first 10 or 12 years extensively covering ground. We drove every passable backroad within a 50-mile radius of home. Then we walked every ridge between those roads. A few great places surfaced. These areas will continue to be productive as long as topography remains constant. Hunting pressure and loss of habitat through development might affect an area somewhat, but one spot is better than another because numerous factors attract deer to these spots.

PRIME PROPERTY: FOOD AND SECURITY

Most great whitetail spots are great because of two things: food and security. Sure, they might offer superior thermal current advantages, tight cover in cold weather, seclusion, ease of movement or a combination of three or more desirable characteristics. There are usually numerous reasons why one spot is better suited for hunting than others. Deer recognize and take advantage of these features. Our job as hunters is to identify these same factors and adjust our plans accordingly. Look for patterns. If you see deer moving a particular way, think about any governing factors. Sun, wind, density of cover, terrain, soil (rocks or dirt), understory, overstory, foliage, temperature, time of day, time of year, rut, food, water, edge, hunting pressure, dogs, light intensity, deer

Little things can mean a lot. Deer prefer particular places to cross obstacles like fences. If you know these tendencies, you're ahead of the game.

41

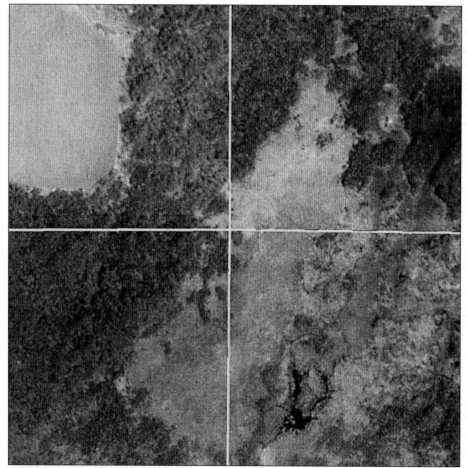
Aerial photos can really show you the lay of the land, saving some footwork.

ing tools that a deer hunter has to work with. Order them from the U.S. Soil Conservation Department located in your county seat. Center the area you're interested in on their master maps. If possible, order the scale that shows one inch equal to 220 yards. It gives exceptional detail. You can actually see individual trees if they stand alone. Framed aerial photos also make great gifts for the landowner.

When your photo comes in, mount it on a piece of cardboard. Cover it with a piece of clear plastic from your local stationery store. Since aerials are usually done in black and white photography, color code the clear plastic with pens. Use different colors to mark roadways, boundaries, feeding areas, bedding cover, major trails, rubs or scrapes, fences—and especially big buck sightings. At the end of the entire season, change to a new piece of acetate. The following year, use the same color codes. After about three years of doing this, superimpose all three plastic sheets to get an accumulation of three years' worth of findings all at once. Patterns, scrape lines, rub lines and trails will jump out at you. Great learning tool. Aerial photos are also super for quickly briefing a hunter on a new area or "plan of attack."

━━◅◙◙◙▻━━

"Aerial photos are one of the most underrated learning tools that a deer hunter has to work with."

━━◅◙◙◙▻━━

numbers, sex ratio, age structure and so on. That's a lot to consider, but all of these things can affect deer movement.

Never be satisfied with your hunting grounds. Nothing is forever. There are places we hunted just 10 years ago that, at the time, we thought would be happy hunting grounds forever. Now, for one reason or another, we don't hunt those places anymore. We've made it a habit to come up with at least one new hunting area every year. It's better to have the problem of not being able to decide where to hunt than to have a situation where you have no good places left.

BIRD'S-EYE VIEW

Life itself goes through cycles. One area might deteriorate for a few years, then come bouncing back better than ever. As hunters, it's our job to keep up. Don't try to depend on memory for detail. We used to write everything down because we had a lot to learn. Now that we're older and smarter (borderline senile), we still write things down so that we don't have to depend on memory. We've both always had a pretty good mind for detail. We like maps and love aerial photos. Aerial photos are one of the most underrated learn-

Don't trust memory. On the wall at camp where we guide, we have all our treestands listed according to time of day and wind direction. Stands should be either named or numbered. One of the first things we do each morning is turn on our weather-band radio. You can buy weather radios for approximately $20. They give 24-hours-a-day weather and wind reports as well as forecasts. We then go to our charts to see which stands are most desirable for the weather conditions. For example, with a northwest wind in the morning, we might try the Bull Pasture stand, Hog Lot or Mosquito Shed

Treestand Safety Commandments

1. Be familiar with all components of your safety equipment and keep them properly maintained and adjusted.

2. Wear a convertible body harness any time your feet are off the ground. Make it a habit to put on your harness first, before doing anything else in your treestand-raising routine.

3. If purchasing a new stand, test it for comfort before you buy. A comfortable stand will help you hunt better and more safely.

4. Read and understand all of the manufacturer's instructions, including caution and warning statements.

5. Practice with your new stand close to the ground before going higher. Always double check to assure good adhesion on the tree, and make sure that all hardware is tight.

6. Be highly skeptical of used and home-made stands. Plus—check your portable stand before putting your full weight on it.

7. Only attach your stand to healthy, straight trees.

8. Before using a limb or branch, ask yourself if you can bet your life on it. Same with tree steps—make sure they penetrate *real wood* and not just bark.

9. Be particularly cautious during inclement weather and icy conditions.

10. Use a rope for raising and lowering your unloaded hunting tool and your pack to and from the stand after you're safely attached to the tree.

— Tom Barnett

Maps can give you a view of the deer woods that you can't get on the ground. By marking these maps each year, you'll start to see trends.

stand. With a southeast wind in the afternoon or evening, we look at Happy's, the Bone Pile Stand, or the Graveyard.

Another scouting tool most hunters neglect is the use of a small plane. Two or three hunting partners can chip in to rent a small plane for a lot less than you'd think. You can cover a lot of ground in even a half-hour flight. Take your camera. Make the top of the lens always point north to avoid confusion. Don't look for deer. Look for habitat, funnels and edges. Take notes such as: "Check small thicket at north end of dike. River has barely visible narrows and riffle just upstream of south point corner ... possible crossing."

Then get out to do your ground work. When we cover new ground, we tend to move at a fairly fast pace, trying to take in as much as possible. Pay no attention to the fact that you might jump deer. We assume that we'll be moving deer as well as disturbing the area, but we don't really mind because we're scouting at this time, not hunting.

When we finally go in to erect a stand, we hope we've put almost all the pieces of the puzzle together via multiple clues. We're most likely already "in the ballpark," but we'll still move any stand for good reason according to visual observations over a period of time.

Time to Move

This is where pride comes in. Sometimes you've simply chosen the wrong spot. Be willing to swallow your pride and move a stand if necessary. Sit a new stand several times to see what happens, then make your decision. Patterns are visible for a reason. Under certain conditions, react accordingly. It's a hunter's job to adapt to the conditions and patterns.

"Be willing to swallow your pride and move a stand if necessary."

More often than not, we find what we figure to be the ideal spot, but there won't be a suitable tree anywhere around for a stand. Don't ever compromise or you'll be defeating your own confidence by selecting what you know in your heart isn't best. Those long hours on stand pass a whole lot quicker if you truly believe you're sitting in the very best spot.

A lot of times we can picture in our minds how a buck enters an area. Pace off certain spots if you have to. Again, think strategy and detail. We believe that trying to imagine a buck's approach better prepares us for what is about to happen. At the same time it confirms that special "feeling" about a given stand, creating not only positive thinking, but positive results.

GOOD GEAR FOR A GOOD SCOUT

by Judd Cooney

Scouting just might be the most significant element of your fall whitetail hunting ventures. Proper scouting techniques can provide you with a wealth of information that will let you plan and execute your fall hunt with confidence and enhance your chances of ending the season with a freezer full of venison and a set of antlers for your den. Proper technique is definitely an important aspect of your scouting ventures to be sure, but equally important is proper scouting equipment.

Everything—from the truck you drive into the countryside to the footgear you wear while hiking the hills—plays an important role in your year-round scouting and can increase the efficiency and effectiveness of your scouting or detract from it, as the case may be.

SCOUTING BY VEHICLE

A thorough discussion of vehicles and their uses in scouting would take a book in itself and still not cover all the bases, so I'll just stick to some of the things that I've learned about vehicle use over the years.

Used conservatively and respectfully, ATVs can serve as useful scouting tools.

Just because you have four-wheel-drive doesn't necessarily mean that you can ride roughshod over private land without giving any thought to the damage you might do. I've met many landowners who have closed their land to hunters because of the damage caused by 4x4s. A set of ruts gouged out of a steep hillside or across a spring-soft pasture or field by a careless, unthinking hunter can lead to serious erosion and NO HUNTING signs on the gates. When you get permission for your scouting and hunting ventures on private property, make sure you get a firm understanding from the landowner as to rules governing the use of vehicles on the property.

Another tip for keeping good relations with the property owners and their neighbors is to keep them informed as to which vehicles you will be using while you are on their land. If I'm driving by a farmhouse on a regular basis in my comings and goings from a hunting area, I will try to stop and let the farmer or his wife know who I am, what I am doing and the vehicles that I will normally be driving. This does much to alleviate their worries and might just give you an in for getting hunting permission in the future. The little courtesies, often overlooked, end up to be important in the long run.

LOW-IMPACT ATV SCOUTING

Used conservatively and with respect for the land, ATVs —either the 2x4s or 4x4s—are also great tools for some serious nonintrusive scouting on a year-round basis. These handy, go-anywhere outfits are popular with anglers, hunters, campers and weekend warriors. Fortunately, they are also extremely popular as working tools for ranchers, farmers, timber cruisers, game and fish personnel and deer hunters. That's definitely a plus when it comes to using them for scouting and for actually transporting hunters into the hunting area.

Deer become accustomed to the sounds of these machines burbling around the woods and fields and probably won't go into a total panic when they hear the sound of one in their area during the middle of the day. On large tracts of public land where ATV use is legal, you can cover a vast amount of country on backroads and trails to check for well used crossings, big tracks, scrapes and rub lines without leaving a smidgen of scent or disturbance on the ground. Once you locate an area with lots of fresh sign, you can really put your scouting techniques to work.

A four-wheel-drive vehicle is by far the most useful equipment-hauling, blind and optics tripod combination available. A 4x4 can get you farther off the beaten path and will keep you in the field longer during inclement weather and in terrain that would bring a two-wheel-drive vehicle to a standstill. Over the years I've made extensive use of both enclosed-interior 4x4s and pickups. I prefer a pickup for hauling equipment such as treestands, ladders, blinds, four-wheelers and snowmobiles. My enclosed-interior rig is great for hauling gear that needs to be kept out of the weather and also serves as a protected place to sleep during many scouting and photo trips. Scouting from your vehicle is often the least intrusive method you can use. A whitetail will tolerate a vehicle several hundred yards away much more readily than it will a person.

"Make sure you get a firm understanding ... as to rules governing the use of vehicles on the property."

46

The four-wheeler's light weight and large, low-pressure tires leave a low-impact footprint, making it ideal for travel in areas where minimum ground or vegetation damage is imperative. Four-wheelers (especially 4-wheel-drive models) are excellent for traveling through heavy bush, timber, swamp or muskeg areas to get off the beaten path where there are fewer hunters and less wary deer. However, these deer probably aren't accustomed to the sounds of these machines, so use your four-wheeler to get back into the area as unobtrusively as possible and then park it and do your serious scouting on foot.

Another advantage of scouting and actually making use of a four-wheeler for hunting is that you don't leave human scent on the ground for a deer to detect. In my hunting and guiding operations, I often prefer to ease a hunter up to a blind or treestand with a vehicle or four-wheeler. I'll drive right up to the treestand or blind, let him exit quietly and then drive off. A vehicle traveling across a meadow or harvested field or down a backroad disturbs deer far less than a human walking or sneaking on foot. A deer spotting a vehicle headed its way will usually just get back into the timber and let it pass. After a few minutes the deer will usually settle down and continue with its normal activities. This might not be the case in areas where there is substantial night hunting and poaching. If a deer spots a hunter sneaking to a stand in the dark or scents the passage of such an intruder, the deer will more than likely vacate the area in short order and let every deer in the area know about it. The only scent trail a hunter traveling to a stand or blind in a vehicle or four-wheeler is going to leave is from the vehicle to the stand. This short trail and small amount of scent is a lot less likely to be detected by a deer's sensitive nose than the scent trail of a hunter walking a quarter mile or more to the stand.

HORSE-TOP SCOUTING

Another method of scouting an area without disturbing deer is by horseback. There are many large tracts of superb whitetail habitat across the nation that just scream for the use of a good saddle horse for efficient, low-impact scouting. You can cover a lot of ground on horseback, locating and working out scrape and rub lines, working your way through bedding areas, traveling and locating the entrance and exit trails and following well used trails to hidden feeding grounds or trees. With a little care, such as wearing clean canvas chaps, rubber boots and gloves, you can do all this and more without disturbing or alerting the local deer population. This fall I will give some serious consideration to making a lot more use of a horse or two for our Iowa whitetail opera-

tion. I can't think of a better way to transport a hunter into a hot buck area and ease him into a treestand, pit or ground blind without leaving scent or spooking deer.

OPTICS: YOU CAN'T SHOOT WHAT YOU CAN'T SEE

It's impossible to think about serious scouting at any time of the year without thinking about good optics. Good binoculars are essential to effective scouting of any type. There is an infusion, or I should say confusion, of new binoculars on

---

"A first-class pair of binoculars indisputably reveals its worth during low-light conditions and periods of extended use."

---

the market that range in price from $10 to $2,500.

I'm always amazed when an ardent whitetail hunter shows up in hunting camp with "el cheapo" binoculars that probably couldn't distinguish between a bull elk and a doe whitetail at 500 yards, even in the bright sunshine of midday. When I ask about his sorry state of optical affairs, he

Scouting atop a horse or mule can be even lower-impact than doing the work on foot.

Do not skimp when it comes to purchasing binoculars. Your eyes will thank you, and you'll see more game.

will leave your eyes feeling like somebody poured sand and salt in them. Determining the trophy aspects of a buck under low-light situations with poor quality glass lenses will leave you mumbling to yourself and cussing the guy who sold you the glasses. The durability of quality binoculars shows up dramatically during extreme heat, cold, moisture and jolts.

CHOOSING BINOCULARS

One of the most important aspects of good scouting binoculars is their twilight factor. This term simply signifies the calculation of the square root of the binoculars' magnification multiplied by the objective lens diameter. The higher the twilight factor, the better the binoculars' light gathering ability for low-light conditions and the easier it will be for you to locate deer and judge a buck's headgear. A good pair of binoculars for hunting and serious scouting should have a twilight factor of at least 15 or higher. Such things as purity of the glass used in the lenses and prisms and the quality of the reflection-reducing lens coatings that maximize light transmission are all factors that affect the overall sharpness of the image you see under adverse scouting conditions.

"A pair of quality glasses will usually provide a lifetime of excellent service and use."

usually states emphatically, "I do all my whitetail hunting in heavy cover and at short distance, so why do I need expensive, large binoculars to haul through the woods or up into a treestand with me?" Scouting! That's why!

Without a decent pair of binoculars it's often tough to distinguish between an average buck and a "boomer" buck in the early morning or late evening light that these antlered phantoms seem to prefer. I wouldn't think of going out scouting without toting the best quality binoculars and spotting scope that I could afford. I'd much rather let my eyes do the walking; it's a lot less tiring. I can cover much more country in less time and I don't make noise or leave a bit of scent to alert a sly, old buck.

Good binoculars are the best combination of magnification, image quality, light-gathering ability, size, weight and durability. Binocular quality is often hard to judge across the counter in a sporting goods store, but a first-class pair of binoculars indisputably reveals its worth during low-light conditions and periods of extended use. Glassing with a set of low quality binoculars for a prolonged period of time

I also prefer central-focusing binoculars—which allow you to fine-tune both oculars simultaneously—rather than individual-focus binocs where you adjust each ocular separately. Center-focus glasses can easily be adjusted to your individual eyesight requirements by independently adjusting the right ocular. One-handed fine-tuning is easily accomplished with center-focus binocs and can be a real pain with individual-focus glasses.

Stay completely away from the "auto-focus" or "stay-focus" binoculars that do not have focusing adjustments. Their price and ease of use might sound appealing, but they are primarily designed for birders and people who only use binoculars sparingly. These binoculars force your eyes to do the focusing or adjusting. After a serious scouting session, when your eyeballs are zooming in and out, focusing and refocusing constantly over a couple hours' time, they're going to feel like they've been sandpapered. For general scouting and hunting, I prefer a set of 7X binoculars. I also make use of a set of 10X glasses when I am glassing from a vehicle or can make use of a solid rest. The lower the magnification, the easier they are to hold steady off-hand.

My vocation as a guide and outfitter necessitates locating deer and other critters before they spot me or my clients. Good optics are a vital part of that function, and I want the best I can afford because they are the most utilized and indispensable tools in my hunting arsenal. A good set of binoculars is certainly not cheap, but a pair of quality glasses will usually provide a lifetime of excellent service and use. I never have figured out the rationale of a serious whitetail hunter who will spend $400 or more on a new bow that will usually only last a few years and then buy the cheapest pair of binoculars available and expect them to give a lifetime of quality use. Good binoculars might well have more to do with the success or failure of his whitetail hunting ventures than his bow.

My personal choice in binoculars has been narrowed to two or three of the sharpest, brightest and most rugged models that I have been able to find. For years I have dangled the Swarovski rubber-armored 7X42mm around my neck on whitetail and other big game hunts across the country. Then I started switching back and forth between them and a pair of Nikon SE 10X42mms that are smaller, lighter and exceptionally bright and sharp. I field-tested a pair of 10X45mm Zeiss Nite Owls that are incredible glasses when it comes to sharpness and light gathering abilities. There are a number of excellent binoculars on the market, so take your time in choosing a pair and you'll be well rewarded for your efforts.

SPOTTING SCOPES

Serious scouting any time of the year also requires a good spotting scope, and there are plenty to choose from. I much prefer a variable power scope of 15X to 45X. I often use the scope on the lower setting to scope distant ridges and areas much like I use binoculars. If I locate a suspicious object, I zoom in on higher power to get a better look. The Swarovski T-80, 20-60X spotting scope is one of the best that I have ever used and is also one of the most expensive. For general spotting in all light conditions, where weight and size are not a factor, I use a 15-45X Nikon ED II Fieldscope. This ultra-sharp scope has the same quality low light dispersion glass in its lenses as my super-expensive Nikon camera lenses. For really long-distance work, I also have a 60X eyepiece that replaces the variable eyepiece. Many a whitetail has been carefully looked over, judged, patterned and recorded for posterity in my notes without ever knowing it was being watched. Where weight is a factor, such as scouting in the backcountry or from the top of a tree, I use a lightweight 16-47X variable power, rubber armored, waterproof, Nikon

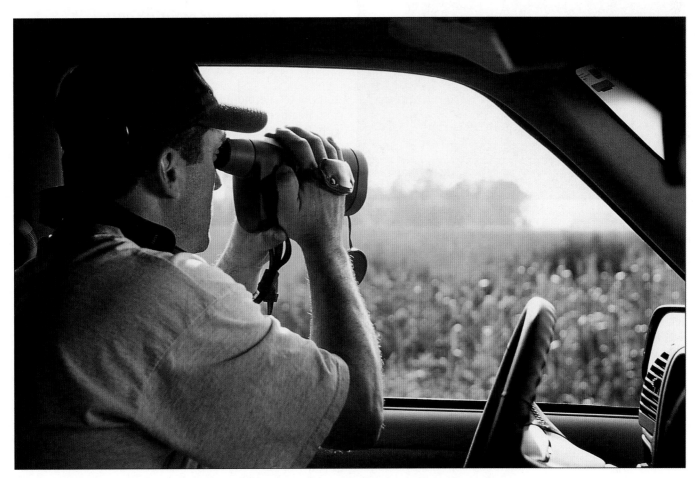

One look through a spotting scope or good set of binoculars tells you that this is a buck worth pursuing.

49

GPS units are fast becoming important tools in the good scout's arsenal.

is made by Bogen and can be bought through a camera store. Bogen also makes a camera mount called the Super Clamp with a swivel head that works great for holding a spotting scope in all sorts of situations. It can be clamped to just about anything and will squeeze the juice out of an oak limb. Don't try to use this clamp on a vehicle window because it can easily break the glass when cranked down.

THE NOTEBOOK

A notebook is another key piece of equipment that should be a constant companion on all your hunting and scouting trips. I am the world's worst when it comes to taking notes, but over my years of dealing with whitetails, my notebooks and the information they contain have proved invaluable. There are several specially designed deer hunting logs on the market, but I just settle for a spiral-bound pad that fits in my

"A good spotting scope is useless without a solid base to hold it steady during your scouting outings."

shirt pocket. Recording such things as deer sightings, buck sizes, weather and wind conditions at stand locations along with dates and time, location of major trails, funnels, travel corridors, signpost rubs and scrapes and the hodgepodge of other information that pops up daily will often keep you from forgetting details that make the difference in your success or failure. When I get back from a scouting trip, I'll transcribe the info from my notebook to my computer for future referencing and study in conjunction with my topo maps and aerial photos.

TECHNO-SCOUTING: GPS

In this age of high-tech equipment, it's only natural that whitetail hunters would find a Global Positioning System (GPS) unit useful in their scouting endeavors. This little hand-held outfit is a real marvel of modern technology that can be used to pinpoint any location in the world. GPS units can be put to good use in scouting to locate the position of such things as various deer sign, springs, saddles, funnels, individual food sources and much more. Several of the GPS units on the market are no larger than a TV remote control and even the larger units will easily fit in a daypack or fanny pack.

These units are fairly simple to operate in the field. The

XL Spotter. Bushnell also makes an excellent line of spotting scopes that are reasonably priced and will more than fill the needs of most whitetail hunters. Redfield, Leupold and Bausch & Lomb also produce superb spotting scopes. Go to a large sporting goods store and compare several scopes until you find one that will fill your needs within your budget.

A good spotting scope is useless without a solid base to hold it steady during your scouting outings. You can build a cheap, reliable scope rest out of a canvas bank money bag or 25-pound shot sack filled with kitty litter. Either will work fine when placed across the hood of your vehicle or on a rock or log. A small, cheap, collapsible tripod available at any camera store is a lot easier to pack around and just as serviceable. Spotting from a vehicle calls for a solid window mount. One of the best lightweight window mounts that I have used first step would be to record your camp, home or some other base of operations as a key waypoint. From there you could head into the field and add individual waypoints consisting of scrapes, funnels, saddle crossings, rub lines, bedding areas or feeding areas. Then accurately transfer this information to your U.S.G.S. maps to give you a better overall view of what's happening in your hunting area. Several GPS units have the capability of downloading info directly into a computer for storage and retrieval when you need it. With this capability you could store data from different areas of the country or hunting camps. When you get ready to head for that area you could load the data into your GPS and the unit would lead you right to each previous waypoint with unbelievable ease.

One of the major deficiencies of some GPS units is their inability to acquire satellite lock-on through heavy overhead cover, which would prevent you from getting a precise reading. In such a situation, you might have to move to the nearest clearing for a reading and then factor in your own offset to get back to that scrape or white oak tree. However, if you purchase a model with a 12 parallel channel receiver, like some of those available from Eagle, Garmin or Magellan, lock-on won't be a problem even in areas with a thick canopy. A GPS unit might be excessive if you are only scouting a 40-acre tract of land behind the barn, but if you are hunting large timbered areas or vast tracts of private or public land and use it enough to realize its capability during scouting situations, you'll never leave home without it. The days of getting lost or not being able to find a specific scrape or feeding area are long gone with a GPS in your pack.

"The days of getting lost or not being able to find a specific scrape or feeding area are long gone ..."

Locking in promising locations on your hand-held GPS can help you keep track of locations to check out later in the season.

REMOTE SCOUTS: MONITORING DEVICES

Unfortunately, proper scouting takes much more time than many hunters are able to give because of the ultra-competitive work world and fast-paced lifestyle they have to endure.

Even those dedicated and fortunate individuals who spend day after day scouting on a year-round basis can't spend 24 hours a day during the two or three months of the season observing whitetail activity.

Learning a whitetail's movement patterns or getting a passing deer's photo during the hours of darkness is often as important to a hunter as knowing the deer's daytime movements. Gaining this information can be a difficult, if not impossible, task using conventional scouting methods. But, again, thanks to modern technology, all is not lost.

My first experience with trail timers or automatic trail monitoring devices of any sort was during bear season when I tried to get a record of a trophy bear that wasn't cooperating by coming to the bait during shooting hours. I used a simple little device called the Trailtimer. This contraption consisted of a small plastic case containing a digital clock, spool of thread, nylon string and a little plastic loop. The clock was set to the correct time with the bottom of the loop shoved into a slot in the clock, depressing the on/off switch and keeping the clock running. I then tied the small unit to a tree near the trail to be monitored. One end of the thread was tied to the bottom of the loop and the other to a solid

object across the animal's route of travel. When the animal hit the thread, the tension before the thread broke pulled the plastic loop out of the clock and stopped it at the exact time that the animal passed. When the thread broke, the broken ends were carried in the direction the animal was traveling.

"This simple, foolproof, pocket-sized device gives the hunter both the time and direction of any passing critter."

This simple, foolproof, pocket-sized device gives the hunter both the time and direction of any passing critter. The Trailtimer is probably used by more deer hunters today than any other trail-monitoring device because of its low price and ease of use.

There are a number of good trail monitoring units on the market today, and you should have no problem finding just the right one for your needs. However, not all of them are the same, nor do they accomplish the same purpose, so it's extremely important for you to decide just how you want to use a trail monitor and what information you need it to provide to increase your knowledge of deer movements. Let me tell you, right up front, that using an electronic trail monitoring device is darn sure not going to give you a lock on getting a trophy buck nor will it let you take unfair advantage of any wary record-class buck. What trail monitors will do is allow you to increase your knowledge of deer movements and habits and possibly provide a photo series of the deer that use a specific trail, scrape or feeding area.

TWO TYPES OF TRAIL MONITORS

There are two basic types of high-tech, infrared trail monitoring devices on the market today.

Remote scouting can really tune you in to your area's deer movement patterns. (Note the trail monitor on the tree to the left of the buck.)

The active infrared monitors make use of two separate units. One is a transmitter that sends out a narrow, invisible beam across the trail, much like stretching out a trip rope across the area to be monitored. The beam is targeted to hit the small sensor in the receiver. Anything that disrupts or breaks this beam will trigger the circuits in the receiver and the time, date and event number will be recorded in the unit's memory. The monitor will also trigger a camera at the same time if the unit is programmed for this function. The unit will store this information until you come along and get a readout. An active infrared beam is sensitive enough to record the passing of a hummingbird but is normally adjusted to a point where only a large animal like a deer will trip it. This eliminates the chance of false readings given by smaller animals or birds passing the monitor. The active infrared's main advantages are its reliability and wide range of sensitivity. Its main disadvantage is the need for two separate units; this means higher initial cost.

Now you can monitor trails—and see what passes by—even when you're not in the woods.

—◁◦◦◦▷—

"The active infrared's main advantages are its reliability and wide range of sensitivity."

—◁◦◦◦▷—

Most of the trail monitors on the market today are passive infrared units. These monitors operate on a heat and motion principle and only need a single unit to monitor an area. The passive infrared monitors throw a series of invisible infrared pulses at intervals across the area to be monitored. Any critter interrupting one or more of these pulses within a given amount of time with its body heat or motion will be registered as an individual event or trigger a camera or both depending on the type of unit.

Single-unit passive monitors are somewhat cheaper than the active units and can be set up under a greater variety of situations. On the other hand, they can be touchier to set up during the hunt because of their broad field of view. Their method of operation can also cause them to record inanimate objects like sun-warmed branches, cornstalks or weeds moving in the midday breeze as events, giving a false activity reading. Once you fully understand how these units work and what they can accomplish under actual field conditions, you shouldn't have any problem setting them up.

The most important step in getting the best "bang for your buck" is to decide just what information you want to obtain from a trail monitoring unit and then find the best outfit for the money that will accomplish your objective. A weekend hunter might want to use one or more units on several deer trails or scrapes during the week to monitor the deer movements. On Friday evening the hunter can check the units to get the dates and times of the week's deer activity. He could study the activity patterns and make optimum use of his limited hunting time on Saturday and Sunday by hunting the trail or scrape that showed the most consistent use during legal hunting hours throughout the week. Some hunters might want to get the same information and also have photos of the deer so he can get a look at their headgear. Another might just be interested in getting deer photos and not so much in getting the times and dates of the deer passing by.

A Photo Album

No doubt about it, motion-sensitive cameras assist in your scouting duties—showing when deer are moving and which ones are doing it. But beyond that functional utility, these units can be just plain fun.

What hunters worth their salt wouldn't get a kick out of discovering the deer that roam their hunting areas? You might see some animals you didn't know live in your area. And you might get some surprise guest appearances to boot. Here are some real-life examples from the camera of NAHC staffer Dave Larsen.

Get to Know the Deer in Your Area

Identify the bucks.

Note daytime movement patterns.

Meet up-and-coming herd members.

Track nocturnal activity patterns.

Enjoy Shots of Some Surprise Visitors

A pheasant rooster walks through.

Wandering raccoons make their presence known.

Some not-so-wild guests appear too.

Even songbirds like this downy woodpecker trigger shots.

When I start working a new area (such as my hunting operation in Iowa), I want to learn as much about the whitetail movements on the lease as efficiently and quickly as I can. Consequently, I use a number of the units—both active and passive—to monitor trails, scrapes, crossings and rublines, throughout the fall hunting season.

I want to know when the deer are crossing between cornfields and the adjacent timber. What changes in their travel patterns occur with the crop harvest or the onset of the rut? What times do deer leave a bedding area and return? What time do they arrive at a holding or loitering area? What increase or decrease in activity in certain areas occurs during the first gun season? When, during the season, are deer most active around waterholes? As the bow season progresses, do they change their patterns from daylight hours to darkness or vice versa? What type of weather conditions trigger heavy use of food plots?

To get as many answers as possible, we set out trail monitors at the start of the season and gather data intermittently throughout the whole season. After closely monitoring a number of key locations over a couple years in our hunting area, we gain some valuable insight into the activities of the local whitetail population. This knowledge makes us better at our scouting craft, and we might even be able to outsmart a trophy buck or two for our clients.

TRAILMASTERS

I started using the Trailmaster monitors a number of years ago. At the time the only models available were the active infrared units. These units would store 1,000 events and run for about a month on a set of four C batteries for each of the transmitter and receiver units. When a camera is attached to the unit you can program the Trailmaster to start taking photos at certain times and stop at specified times. Bill Goodson, the designer of the units, has since brought out a passive unit that will also take a camera hookup and has specified starting and stopping times for the camera's operation. All Trailmaster units have full adjustment for the sensitivity of the pulses and the timeframe in which they must be broken. All of the units are waterproof and will operate at any temperature encountered in the field.

The Trailmaster series also has a plug-in for a small data printer so you can get a printed readout from your Trailmaster unit in the field by simply plugging in a connecting cord and touching a couple of buttons.

Trailmaster also has a data collector unit and a computer program that allows a hunter with several of these units out in the woods to carry the collector into the field, plug it into the trail monitor, push a couple of buttons and dump the data from the monitor into the collector, all in the blink of an eye. You can gather data from as many as 16 different monitors and then transfer this data to your computer at home. You can then merge it with previous data from the same location and get a printout of the data

in graph or printed form. With the Trailmaster units it's possible to store a whole season's data in your computer to be studied at your leisure. These units are for the serious deer hunter and will add a whole new dimension to your learning about whitetail habits.

TRAILTIMERS

Trailtimer, mentioned earlier, offers an easy-mounting, passive unit that will record and store 500 events and operates on one 9-volt battery. This unit has a small focused circular beam, three feet in diameter at 60 feet. This configuration helps to eliminate false signals and faulty data. The unit does not have a camera hookup; however, this unit is compatible with Trailtimer's TT 2000 camera system. They also lack printer ports and data dump capabilities, but these units will likely fit the budget of most whitetail hunters.

The Deerfinder Game Monitor, manufactured by Non-Typical Engineering, is a unique piece of equipment in many ways. The monitor itself is a rugged, compact, black ABS plastic unit. Its main weight comes from the single D-cell battery used to power the unit for up to four months. The unit will record up to 500 events and can also be used in conjunction with a camera to get a photo of the critter tripping the monitor. Similar to other passive monitors, the Deerfinder uses a cone-shaped beam that will detect an animal's body heat out to approximately 60 feet under ideal conditions. The similarity stops when you pick up the calcu-

"These units ... will add a whole new dimension to your learning about whitetail habits."

lator-sized keyboard that accompanies the Deerfinder monitor. This little keyboard is the brains of the outfit and turns the detector unit on and off, sets it in either Deerfinder mode, where it simply monitors and records deer movements, or in DeerCam mode, where it records events and trips the connected camera.

This little unit also is distinctive in that the detector unit can be protected by a password so that only you can turn it on or off. (This feature was designed to discourage someone from stealing the monitor.) The Deerfinder unit also has an adjustable event delay control, which means that you can adjust the time after an event is recorded before it will record another event. This precludes getting 100 event recordings of a buck making a scrape. Most preset units operate on a one-event-per-minute basis, but with this unit you can vary the time from one to 99 seconds or from one to 99 minutes. The Deerfinder also allows the user to program in a certain time-

Tips and Techniques: Trail-Monitoring Units

Most of these trail-monitoring units operate in much the same way, and things that create a problem for one unit will probably create a problem for others as well. After several years of utilizing these devices, I have probably made every mistake known to man and come up with several that were entirely new. Practice with the monitors in the off-season so you are completely familiar with their operation and the little things that can give you false information.

Here are some things I've learned that might save you some time and frustration:

1. Always fasten the monitors to solid objects. A moving base will often cause the unit to trigger and give you a mass of false readings.

2. Keep the units in the shadows and out of direct sunlight to avoid false readings.

3. Make sure there are no major movable objects in the unit's field of view that can change temperature as the day warms up or can move in the breeze to give false readings.

4. Keep the units level so you get maximum and equal coverage of the activity zone.

5. If you're using a camera with your monitor, make sure the unit and the camera are compatible. Some of the newer cameras go into a "sleep" mode after a period of inactivity and the unit's circuitry might not be capable of turning the camera back on.

Electronic trail monitors aren't going to guarantee you a shot at a big buck, but they can broaden your knowledge of deer activity and habits. This type of knowledge is often your best defense against getting "whupped" day in and day out by an old whitetail buck.

---

frame when the camera can be activated. It can also be programmed to operate 24 hours a day. The user can also control the camera delay sequence, the same as with the event delay sequence, and program the camera activity to take a single photo or two photos two seconds apart.

When recording events, the Deerfinder will record up to 500 events and then continue to record the most recent event and delete the first (oldest) event, thereby giving you access to the most up-to-date event. With the keyboard unit you can read through the events by using up and down scrolling keys or you can use the auto recall button to bring the event up on the screen for a couple of seconds and then it will scroll on to the next event.

Cameras

Many hunters are strictly interested in getting photos of the deer they have been hunting all season. For them the CamTrakker might be just the ticket. This unit consists of a passive infrared sensor unit connected to an autofocus, autowind, autoflash 35mm camera—all housed in a waterproof ABS plastic housing. The whole unit fastens to a tree, post or other solid object overlooking a trail, scrape or feeder. You simply set the unit to operate the camera continuously, day only or night only, set the delay between photos to one of the three options—either three, six or 10 minutes—and

you are in business. The camera has a date-and-time feature so when you get the photos back from the processor you will know when the photo was taken. This unit is a simple and relatively foolproof way to get photos of the critters you are chasing around the woods.

Gearing Up For Scouting: A Summary

We've covered a lot of ground here—and that somehow seems appropriate when the subject is scouting. Like the far reaches of this story, you have to reach out when you scout in order to decipher where the big bucks live, what they did last fall and what they might be doing this fall.

Of course, you have to reach out to cover many miles of ground—that's where trucks, ATVs, horses and optics come into play. But you also need to search far and deep within the areas you select to hunt—that's when you can use GPS units, trailtimers, remote cameras and the other high-tech equipment.

Is it all fair, all this gear, when all the whitetail has are its acute senses and survival instincts, along with an intimate knowledge of its home range? I think you have the answer right there. When it comes to bagging a good buck, the name of the game is preparation, and scouting forms that core. If you get out there and do the work, using good gear in a good scouting plan, you deserve the buck.

IT NEVER ENDS

by Judd Cooney

> *"Back to square one … scouting!"*

As you've read throughout this chapter, scouting is the key to making your hunting season a "lead pipe cinch." All you have to do is spend a couple of days locating a good buck, determine where he is moving during the early morning and late evening hours, slip into his core area and put up a treestand overlooking one of his trails. Wait a few days for the season to open and let things quiet down in the woods. Sneak into your stand in the predawn darkness on opening day and shoot the buck when he comes walking by an hour later. Ohhh! Were it only so easy and assured, I probably wouldn't need to be writing this. And I probably wouldn't have a job as a whitetail outfitter. No one would need me.

Unfortunately, or fortunately, depending on your perspective, most of us find ourselves still out in the woods well into the season, wondering just how the hell we are going to get a deer close enough to shoot with only a month of the season left. Back to square one … scouting!

Early in the season, especially if you're a bowhunter or muzzleloader hunter, you are going to be hunting bucks that are after food and undisturbed bedding time. The only way to take one of these beasts is to pattern him on his way to and from the bedding area. Occasionally, this is a simple process and you can get lucky. Quite often, the largest bucks will simply disappear and you might never see them again in that particular area. Because of the terrain, habitat or layout of the crops in the area, a mature buck can pull a disappearing act with ease during early fall and the pre-rut.

You might be concentrating your hunting efforts and spending time in a treestand. But never let up on your scouting efforts even when sitting on your butt. During this period of the season you'll probably do most of your hunting early mornings and late evenings, when the reclusive bucks are a bit more active. While you're sitting in the stand, keep your binoculars in action, scouting, especially if you see deer movement. I can't understand how a hunter can sit on any stand or stalk through the woods or prairies without constantly making use of a good set of binoculars. If you see deer moving in the woods or in the open, pinpoint exactly where the deer move through the heavy cover into the feeding area or cross an open field or disappear into cover, when they leave the feeding ground. As soon as you quit hunting in the morning, when it warms up and the deer have quit moving, leave your stand and spend an hour or two thoroughly scouting the area. If you spot deer in the evening, mark the location in your memory or notebook and return after hunting the following morning. You might be surprised at the unobtrusive and unlikely locations of trails and travel corridors that you might have missed on earlier scouting trips or new ones that weren't active when you scouted the area previously.

"Scouting can make the difference between simply watching deer ... and getting a shot at a buck."

If a good buck appears from the same location more than once, you had better be carefully scouting for a new stand location—right now! Aggressive and continuous scouting can often make the difference between simply watching deer in frustration and getting a shot at a buck.

ALTERED HABITAT

As the season progresses and the farmers and ranchers begin harvesting their crops and reducing vast areas of heavy cover into barren stubble fields, there is a drastic change in deer habits. Continual in-season scouting is necessary to keep you constantly aware of current deer locations. This can be a real problem in many areas because the protective cover provided by crops can change on a daily basis. An important part of your in-season scouting should be to stay in contact with locals such as school bus drivers, rural mail carriers, trappers, pheasant hunters, farmers and ranchers to get the latest input on their deer (especially big buck) sightings.

Another tactic that will give you lots of information on in-season deer movements, whether it is early in the season or during the rut, is what I term "cruise scouting."

You can scout from home some too ... with a map and some friendly phone calls.

When I have clients in the field hunting, I cruise the roads in the general area or even a totally new area, concentrating on tracks crossing the road. When I find a likely crossing with lots of sign, I scout out the area for hunting potential and check on the landowner status of the adjacent lands. I'll usually brush out all the tracks and make a note of the date in my ever-present notebook. The next time I cruise through the area I'll check the crossing again. If it's still being hammered by deer traffic, I'll get serious about finding a place back off the road to locate a stand. This is also an excellent type of location to make use of an electronic trail monitor (see "Good Gear for a Good Scout" in this chapter).

A CASE STUDY

One year during our preseason scouting we located a monstrous 160-class buck along with several other Pope and Young Club contenders that were using a small, overgrown area of hawthorn, sumac and snowberry as an alternate bedding area. This patch was off the beaten path in the center of a mile-square section. It was well hidden at the bottom of a sloping, bowl-shaped depression, bordered by a narrow treeline that separated the bedding ground from several large cornfields.

Options for a treestand were limited to one questionable-sized box elder tree on our side of the fence. When we first checked it out and discovered numerous beds and fresh rubs, we mounted an electronic trail monitor to cover the main trail leading into the area along with a portion of the bedding ground. Over a period of a week, the monitor readout showed that the deer were moving from the cornfield to the bedding ground around 8 or 9 a.m. and leaving the patch between 4 and 6 p.m. on a somewhat sporadic basis. We hunted the patch several times and passed easy shots on some smaller bucks, but the monster never showed.

I contacted the owner of the adjacent property to get permission to hunt from the treeline on his property. During our conversation, I found out that he and his crew were planning to harvest the adjacent cornfields the following day. In-season scouting is gathering information any way possible that can help put you in the right place at the right time. By learning of the farmer's upcoming harvest plans, I had a darn good chance to make the most of a promising situation.

The following morning I put one hunter in the brush

"Knowing when and how a farmer is going to work his field can give you a great chance to waylay a good buck."

Shed antlers: Proof positive that a buck survived the previous hunting season and should still be running in the territory.

patch bedding area and another covering a well-used trail along the top of a timbered hillside, bordering the upper end of the cornfield. I told both hunters that they were there for the duration of the day or until the combine was done. I figured that sooner or later during the day the combine would get down to the last few rows, and the deer that had been living in the corn all fall would have to vacate and hopefully give one of our hunters a chance.

It's always a good bet to spend some of your in-season scouting checking with farmers to learn when they plan to harvest their crops. I missed a record-class buck in Illinois several years ago, as he broke out of the last few rows of a field the farmer was picking. The farmer told me that he had seen some good bucks in this field and gave me permission to set up on top of a hill where he figured the deer would cross on their way from the field to the nearest heavy woods. Any number of farmers have told me that most deer will simply move over in the field as the combine approaches and normally won't break for the nearest cover until there are only 10 to 20 rows left in the field. Knowing when and

Knowing crop harvest plans can help you harvest a buck ... if you've scouted thoroughly.

how a farmer is going to work his field can give you a great chance to waylay a good buck as he tries to head for the protection of the nearest heavy cover.

THE PAYOFF

By noon the cornfield was about half harvested, so I decided to check on my hunters to find out if they had seen any activity. The hunter covering the bedding area was totally bored, having only seen one pheasant. He was a savvy, trophy whitetail hunter and figured we were on the right track, so he decided to spend the rest of the afternoon in the tree overlooking the bedding ground. The bowhunter on the hill was another story. He could hardly speak when I eased up to his treestand. An hour earlier a monstrous 10-point, that the hunter figured would score more than 190, had walked out of the corn and stood on the trail he was covering at a distance of 80 yards. The humongous buck then moved along the edge of the cornfield and disappeared 50 yards farther down the ridge, leaving my client in a state of shock. Needless to say, I couldn't have dragged the hunter out of the tree at that point.

When I picked the hunters up that evening, the hunter on the ridge had passed on a small eight-point. The hunter in the bedding area hadn't seen a thing until 4 p.m., when a heavy 10-point that would have scored 160 walked over the hill from the opposite direction and bedded down in the weed patch 75 yards away. The buck was completely hidden in the heavy growth and, as far as the hunter was aware, the buck was still there when it got dark and I came to pick him up. Sometimes even good information and the best laid plans don't work when you're dealing with whitetails. But we were certainly on the right track.

RUT SCOUTING

When the rut is in full swing during the season, your best bet is to stay in the woods all day—hunting and scouting. The bucks are liable to be anywhere at any time, and by staying out or scouting from daylight to dark you are going to increase your chances of an "up-close-and-personal" encounter with one of them.

The main thing to remember during the rut is to be mobile and flexible; don't hunt the same stand or area day-in and day-out if you aren't seeing bucks. Hunt your favorite stands or areas morning and evening, but cover some new

60

country during the middle of the day, trying to locate a buck on the move. If you see a good buck, get after him; either hunt him right then and there, or scout out the area where you spotted him and try to find a stand location to hunt from.

"Don't get so overanxious that when you find a surefire spot you stop looking."

When you're scouting during the season don't get so overanxious that when you find a surefire spot you stop looking. Carefully check the surrounding area for an even better place because there just might be a fresher scrape or rub over the next ridge or a better trail down the next draw.

Failing to follow my own advice probably cost me a 150-class buck several years ago. I had been bowhunting for a week and wasn't seeing the buck I knew was in the area. So I expanded my scouting to take in a stretch of public land that I knew harbored a couple of good bucks. The first day I found a well-used, small cornfield that was being worked pretty heavily. I aimed to find a location off the field nearer to a bedding area, so I scouted out the section of timber on the ridge above the field. I found lots of rubs along the edge of the woods and a number of scrapes that were being worked. I picked a spot in a corner of the woods overlooking a weed-filled tree plot that looked as if it served a dual purpose as a bedding area and travel corridor between the woods. I was above the field and a more extensive section of timber across the flat. There were five active scrapes along the edge of the woods near the corner, numerous rubs on the young trees in the plot and several well-used trails emerging from the timber into the weed/tree patch. I stuck up a portable treestand and figured I was going to kill a good buck there in a couple of mornings or evenings ... wrong!

I saw several does and a 150-class buck cross the weed patch and enter the timber 75 yards above me, but I was so sure I had picked just the right place I didn't bother to check the area into which the deer crossed. After a few unsuccessful

When you're not on stand, be mobile and flexible during the rut. Cover new country and look for better sign, better hunting locations.

days, I let a friend of mine hunt the stand and he arrowed a doe standing on the scrape just at dark, while he was listening to a buck grunting and raking a tree just behind the stand. The next day when we went to get the doe, I discovered that the trail past the stand followed the ridge through a small saddle where a number of small trees had been recently rubbed and thrashed bare and intersected another trail that paralleled the edge of a deep draw. This well-traveled trail was lined with big rubs and numerous fresh scrapes. It was then obvious that the big buck had been sticking to the heavy timber and was simply circling behind my stand on the edge of the open, at least during the daylight hours. The following day, I moved the stand to the junction of the trails, but due to business commitments, I never got to hunt the area again. You can bet that's one place I am going to check out this coming fall, and you can be sure that I'm not going to assume that either location where I had the stands last fall is the best place until I thoroughly scout the whole area this time.

Do a complete job of scouting your entire area. Sleeper hotspots seem to stay hidden for a reason.

There is a narrow line that separates adequate in-season scouting to keep you hunting the best areas and over-scouting that defeats your purpose by driving wary deer out of the area. Only experience and a continual lack of success will tell you when you've crossed this very narrow line.

CAN YOU REALLY PATTERN DEER?

by Charles J. Alsheimer

I wish I had a dollar for every time someone has said to me, "All summer I watched a beautiful buck in a nearby clover field. He came out like clockwork every evening. Then in early fall he disappeared. Where did he go? Can you tell me what happened?"

Patterning whitetails is a subject that I've thought about and studied extensively for years, and it's a topic of particular interest to today's deer hunters. During the course of a year, hunters are bombarded with articles pontificating on how to pattern individual bucks. Often when I read such articles, I find myself asking, "Who's kidding whom?" For the hunter who prefers to hunt whitetails in October and November, the chances of patterning a particular buck remind me of what it takes to win the lottery. It's simply not as easy as many "experts" would like you to believe.

ANNUAL PATTERNS

Biologically speaking, a whitetail buck becomes a totally different animal when October arrives in the North. From the time a buck sheds his antlers in winter until he peels velvet in late August, his testicular volume and serum testosterone levels are low. For this reason bucks do not show a great deal of aggression and tend to have a small home range, often little more than one square mile in size. In

Defining patterns requires hard work, both in the field and on paper.

September, the testicular volume and serum testosterone levels begin increasing rather significantly, bringing on a number of rutting characteristics—one of which is an increase in the size of a buck's range.

The size of a whitetail's area, or range, depends on where it lives. Studies have shown that whitetails living in relatively open habitat tend to have larger home areas than those living in eastern farm country. Also, the home ranges of bucks tend to be much smaller when there is a high doe population.

For example, in the farmland region of the Northeast, where there is adequate woodland cover, a white-tailed buck often spends much of his year in a one-square-mile area. Then when October arrives and eases toward November's rut, a buck's range might balloon to three or four times the size of his summer range. Depending on the animal, this could represent an increase of anywhere from two square miles to several square miles.

At this point the breeding urge begins to overpower a buck, and he goes wherever his nose tells him to go. This means he checks every doe group in his expanded area. In the process he curtails his eating habits, grabbing only a nibble here and there. Attempting to figure out where a buck is feeding during this time is, at best, anyone's guess. With increased movement comes decreased predictability. In an

"The home ranges of bucks tend to be much smaller when there is a high doe population."

attempt to find an estrous doe, a buck might travel in a very irregular pattern for up to five or six hours before bedding. During these forays he might make from five to 12 scrapes an hour. He's truly "on the fly." When this happens, any hopes of patterning that buck are cast to the wind. He's no longer a creature of habit.

PATTERNING OBSTACLES

In spite of this, I do believe that under certain conditions whitetail bucks can be patterned. Patterning means different things to different people. To me it means being able to view the buck in question consistently at least every four days during daylight hours. In my mind, anything more than four days isn't patterning. It's a game of chance.

The circumstances that greatly improve the ability to pattern are: 1) a very limited or centralized food source (i.e., baiting) where an adequate number of doe family groups exist; 2) deer being forced into a confined area (i.e., Western river-bottoms, urban settings or a large high-fenced operation); 3) being able to hunt a buck early in the fall (August or September) when there is a very defined bedding and feeding area and before his hormone level causes him to begin moving and 4) hunting during the post-rut when the buck in question has returned to his core area and there is a preferred food source nearby.

KEYS TO PATTERNING

At best, patterning a specific whitetail buck outside of the circumstances listed above is a "crap shoot." And even then there are specific keys that a hunter will have to know about to be successful at patterning.

Access
The vision of patterning and killing a particular buck can be exciting. But when reality sets in, the thought of what it takes to hunt a buck with a four-square-mile rutting range creates a host of obstacles, the biggest of them access to the land he's covering. For this reason, access to hunting land just might be the major key to patterning and hunting a particular buck.

Buck-to-Doe Ratio
Though they should, the dynamics of buck-to-doe ratios seldom enter into a conversation about patterning. This is a critical factor in being able to successfully pattern a whitetail buck. The closer the buck-to-doe ratio is to one antlered buck for every adult doe, the greater a mature buck's travel pattern. Fortunately for most deer hunters in America, this is not the case. When there are many adult does for every antlered buck, the amount of territory that a buck covers is diminished greatly, especially if there are well-defined doe family groups in a given area.

Great Food Source
As the saying goes, "Find the food source, find the buck." There's no question that knowing what foods are being consumed at specific times during the fall will increase the chances of successfully patterning a given buck. The key is knowing what's "hot" at a specific point in time. This is not always easy because whitetails can be picky eaters. Sure, they'll eat lots of different types of forage, but they will gravitate to preferred food sources. One day they might be piling into a clover field, and three days later they'll switch to browsing on honeysuckle leaves. For this reason, it's important to study available habitat closely to see where the doe family groups are feeding. In areas where baiting is legal,

The rut, and chasing does, enlarges a buck's range and makes him harder to pattern.

hunters can create their own "honey holes" rather easily. Though controversial, this is a technique that's used successfully to pattern deer.

Moon Phase

Up until five or six years ago not much thought was given to the impact moon phases have on patterning whitetails. There's now been enough excellent research done to know that whitetails are more active during a full and three-fourths moon phase than any other. It behooves deer hunters to become "moon watchers" because of the increased daytime deer activity during these two moon phases, especially when they occur during November.

Weather

Along with moon phase, weather has a distinct impact on the movement patterns of whitetails, especially during the rutting period. This entire story could be filled with the ins and outs of how whitetails move during specific weather patterns. The important thing to remember is that deer movement will increase significantly when the barometric pressure is rapidly falling or rising. Also, if a high-pressure system moves in after a storm system has passed through an area, there will be a period of high deer activity. If this occurs during a November full moon period, activity will be higher than during non-rutting months.

Region of the Country

Having hunted whitetails extensively throughout North America, I'm acutely aware that patterning whitetails in certain regions is easier than others. In areas of the Northeast, where baiting is illegal, the thought of patterning a whitetail is but a "pipe dream." In places like New York's Adirondack Mountains and Maine's famed Allegash region, the deer population is so low that a buck's territory is extremely large. On the other hand, in the riverbottoms of the Midwest and West, whitetails can be fairly predictable because their bedding areas are so confined. So, the ability to pattern deer varies from region to region.

Hunting Pressure

Now for the kicker. The ability to pattern whitetail bucks during the autumn months is proportional to the amount of hunting pressure an area gets. If the area has no hunting pressure, patterning is possible. If hunting pressure is high, the chance of seeing a mature buck moving during daylight is virtually unheard of. A whitetail buck with more than two hunting seasons under his belt adapts rapidly to the presence of man and knows when the woods are safe. As hunting pressure increases, bucks quickly become more and more nocturnal.

Actual Hunting Time

Lack of time to hunt is also a critical factor in one's ability to pattern a white-tailed buck. The majority of deer hunters only have the chance to hunt weekends. This means that most deer hunters can only hunt 10 or so days a year, at best. This, in and of itself, makes patterning virtually impossible for the majority of whitetail hunters. So, do you still want to try patterning whitetails?

WINNING THE CHESS MATCH

There have been years when I've scouted a specific buck throughout the summer and have been fortunate enough to cross his path during the season and take him. But to me, this isn't patterning. This scenario falls into the category of knowing how to hunt and being in the right place at the right time.

About the only way to keep tabs on a buck after the second week in October (if you can at all) is by monitoring the doe groups. Unlike bucks, does live in the

Sure sign of a buck. But during the rut, he won't be home often.

same area throughout the year and seldom increase their range during the rut. Because of a buck's unpredictability during the rut, I gravitate to the doe groups in hopes of intercepting a buck that I've seen before. When the breeding begins, there is a good chance that a given doe or group of does will hold him, especially if the does live in a buck's core area. By knowing where the doe groups bed, eat and how they move between the bedding and feeding areas, I've been able to get second or third glimpses of bucks I've watched during the summer. Again, this isn't truly patterning. But it's close. And it's often the tactic that helps me fill my tag with a mature buck.

For the most part, I prefer to hunt in a natural funnel (between the bedding and feeding areas) as close to the bedding area as possible. With this kind of setup, I've experienced good activity during both morning and evening sits. Generally, this kind of funnel will be a prime scraping area for bucks during the chase phase of the rut that occurs just before the breeding begins. The beauty of locating such an area is that it will remain hot even when the breeding commences. In spite of being in estrus, a doe will continue to move and feed and, in many cases, this movement will be more frequent because a doe is more active when she approaches and enters estrus. Often when a hot doe heads for the feeding area, she'll have a love-sick buck in tow.

Once the rut is over and bucks begin to lose interest in does, patterning again becomes a possibility. When a buck's testosterone level drops, he will start reverting to his pre-rut behavior. Unfortunately, a buck that has survived the rigors of both the rut and a long gun season usually becomes totally nocturnal. The key is to hunt the funnel areas in an attempt to ambush a buck as it comes to feed. With an innate drive to add weight lost from the rut, bucks can often become very predictable.

FINAL WORDS

Patterning whitetails is no easy feat. After years of trying to pull it off, I can offer this piece of advice: Rather than trying to scout and hunt one particular animal, try to learn all you can about all the bucks and does in your area. Doing so will allow you many more options when opening day rolls around. And knowing that there are several nice bucks in the

Natural funnel areas will attract does, rutting activity ... and bucks.

area allows you to be more selective. Seldom do I recommend hunting one animal. Hunting is supposed to be fun, not pressure-packed, and I assure you that nothing is more frustrating than trying to hunt a seasoned whitetail buck with several autumns under his belt. Find an area with several good bucks and play the percentages.

Once the pre-rut ends, a buck's range increases significantly. In most cases, a buck's home range will be elongated. Linear home ranges are often a result of an animal maximizing available resources while minimizing movement and energy expenditure. Also, natural features like ridgelines and water can influence the linear makeup of a buck's home range. In a Moore/Marchinton study, the study buck's home range was more than six miles long; this illustrates how active a buck becomes during the rut.

Chapter 3

THE HUNT IS ON

Opening day can be make-or-break, or simply the start to a three- or four-month effort. During gun deer seasons in many of the popular deer hunting states like Pennsylvania, Wisconsin and Michigan, more than 50 percent of all the deer taken with firearms fall during that precious opener. The tally drops dramatically each day following. The time is now—especially if you have your sights set on an old buck.

If, on the other hand, you also hunt with a bow and/or muzzleloader, August, September or the first part of October might not put you in any great hurry. There's time to plot strategy, save a stand for the perfect wind, fine tune a buck's entry and exit of a particular field, try him far from his bedding area so that you don't mess him up before the rut. Decisions, decisions.

That's what it all really boils down to now. Which stand? Decoy or no decoy? Rattle? Grunt? Shut up? It's a feel for whitetails that comes mostly as the result of lessons learned from painful mistakes.

In this chapter you'll read about some of the miscalculations that even the "pros" make. And, with any luck, you'll learn from both these and the success stories to come. You've paid your dues by scouting and dedicating the hours to familiarizing yourself with the lay of the land. Gun hunter or bowhunter, the time is now; the hunt is on.

Good reading, and good luck ...

PLAYING THE ODDS

by Bill Winke

Y ou have to base your deer hunting decisions on something. I like to base mine on how my odds for success are affected. Some steps that you take can have a huge impact on your odds. Don't overlook a single one of them.

LOCATION

In trophy hunting, as in real estate, location is everything. Before you can pick the right tree, you have to pick the right property. And in some cases, the quest might even take you to a different county, state or country. This is the hunt before the hunt, and it is the most difficult part of trophy hunting. No amount of stealth and woodsmanship will make up for an area devoid of big bucks. Most consistently successful trophy hunters are good woodsmen, but I'll guarantee you that all of them hunt the very best places they can find.

Finding the best hunting areas is hard, time-consuming work. You need to talk to a lot of people and walk a lot of ground before you know the absolute best spots to hunt each season. Good farms and bad farms are often found within a mile of each other. And things change from year to year depending upon crop rotation, as well as the success rates and hunting practices of the local bow and gun hunters.

If there are three good bucks on a 300-acre farm, your odds of tagging one are roughly three times better than on a similarly sized farm where there is only one. It's that simple. Once you've identified a hotspot, do what you have to do (short of trespassing, of course) to get on there.

I've put up tens of thousands of hay bales and planted fenceposts until my hands bled, just to gain and keep hunting rights. As a result, I've made some great friends and I've never lost access to a single good piece of ground once I've gained it. These days, I hunt the absolute best places that I can find in several different states. There are a lot of sacrifices involved in getting there. Regardless of what you might think, excellent hunting areas are still available for those willing to look hard ... and work hard.

STAND PLACEMENT

Several springs ago I found a good rubline along the side of a ridge while scouting. That fall I grabbed a portable stand and went back. The rubline had been reworked, and without considering my options further, I simply put up the stand and began waiting. Before the day was over a really nice 10-pointer had given me the slip.

I knew even as I was putting the stand up that I was violating my number one rule in stand placement, but I was too lazy that day to exert the teaspoon of extra effort it would have taken to get that buck. This rule is simple: Never put up a stand to cover only one travel route when you can cover two. Never cover only two when you can cover three and so on. Day-in and day-out, it is a simple rule that makes a big difference.

Decisions, decisions. Choosing the right tree is an art learned through many years of experience and the frustrations of bucks walking past out of range.

71

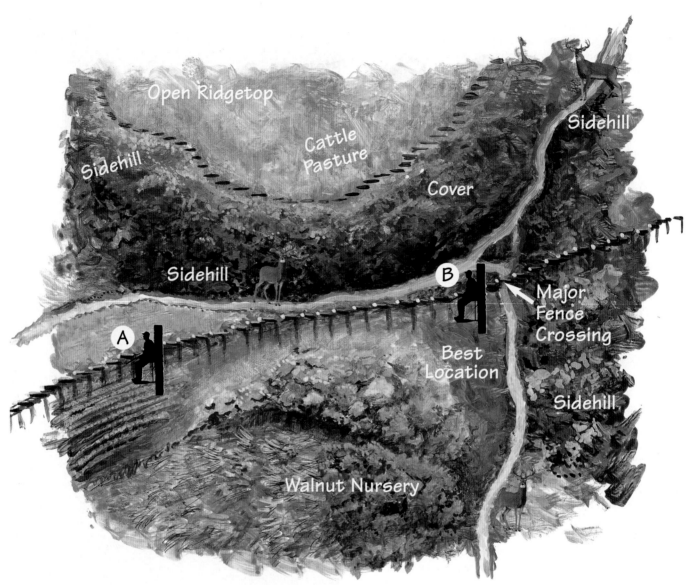

A simple rule of stand placement: Never cover only one travel route when you can cover two or more. While stand A is not in a bad spot, stand B is a much better location: You can cover deer following the fenceline as well as deer using the fence crossing.

I should have slipped along the rubline until I came to a position that would also have allowed me to cover the ridge-top trail without giving my wind away. It wouldn't have been a tough stunt because I knew that the ridge-top trail would be there. The big buck slipped past just out of range two hours after I set up the stand. That buck reinforced a central theme in trophy strategy: Never quit looking for ways to improve your odds. It seems that painful lessons are the best teachers.

Here's one that's even more painful. During a season several years ago, I helped my buddy Mike pick out a spot for his treestand. We wanted to get in and out quickly, without leaving a lot of scent, so we didn't check things out as well as we should have. We picked what seemed like a good spot. From that stand Mike saw several impressive bucks, each just out of range. The clincher came near the end of

the rut, however.

A rack the likes of which he'll never see again came bobbing up the fenceline—heading directly toward Mike. According to my friend, the 12-point typical had at least a two-foot inside spread, great mass and better than foot-long tines. The mighty buck was a legend maker. Instead of continuing along the fence, right past Mike's drawn bow, he stopped 60 yards away. The buck looked around for a few moments before jumping the fence. Mike will never forget the sight of those huge antlers floating easily over the barbed wire and disappearing forever in the weed field beyond.

That world-class buck taught us two tough lessons. Mike was covering a fenceline that comprised only one travel route. (Remember my number one rule of stand placement?) We should have looked up and down the fence until we came to the perpendicular trail that the buck had used. In hindsight, it was an obvious thing to see. The trail was there as big as day. Mike still would have been covering the fenceline and would have had a possible world record right in his lap.

The second lesson is just as important. If you are going to put up a stand that you will be using several times during the season, make sure you get the job done right the first time. What you gain by leaving the few extra tracks required to find a high-odds stand location far outweighs the negative effects of a little additional human scent left behind.

— oɔ∕ɔo —

"Never put up a stand to cover only one travel route when you can cover two."

— oɔ∕ɔo —

What if there was one tree on each of the pieces of property you hunt that every big buck eventually has to walk past? Trying to find it will change the way you think about your hunting area. What you'll find are better stand sites than any you've sat in before—spots where your odds will really skyrocket. The trick is knowing what constitutes a big buck travel route, but we'll get to that later in this book. First we need to look at some more ways to up your odds.

SHOOTING LANES

Rod Ponton lives to bowhunt big whitetails in his home state of Kansas. Rod has hunted several truly giant whitetails in the past decade, but none can compare to the one he almost took several years ago. Rod saw a tremendous typical from a treestand and slipped along the ground to within 60 yards of the buck. He was awesome! A 10-pointer with incredible mass, width and tine length. No stranger to big bucks, Rod is sure that the G-4s (fourth point on each beam) were still well over 12 inches in length! There's no telling what that buck would've scored, but the fact that he was framed up as a potential world-record contender cannot be denied.

The following season, Rod hunted that buck and only that buck. "He was following a doe when I saw him again in the middle of November that second year," Ponton says. "They were both coming down a trail, and they were breathing hard like they had been doing a lot of chasing. The doe stopped short and the buck goosed her. She trotted right past the hedge tree I was sitting in, perfectly through my shooting lane. Instead of following her, the buck went on the other side of the tree, away from the trail. I didn't have a shooting lane in that direction, so all I could do was watch.

He was only about 12 yards away. I could have spit on him, but I had no shot. I never saw him again after that."

What would my friend have given for an opening to shoot through on the opposite side of the twisted hedge tree? The simple decision of whether or not to open another shooting lane can have more to do with tagging a trophy than how well you handle your gun or bow.

Several seasons ago I climbed into an afternoon stand. Going over all the possible shot opportunities and how I would handle each one, I kept coming back to one area in front of me where I had no possible shot. After sitting in the stand for more than an hour, I couldn't take it any longer. I climbed down and cleared two wrist-thick saplings and a couple of low limbs. I was quickly back up in the tree. Within an hour a great buck stopped momentarily right in that opening. I got him, but had I not earlier trimmed out the lane, I wouldn't have been able to shoot. Your ability to cover the area around your stand has a tremendous effect on your odds for success. Though they might try, no one can tell you which side of the tree a trophy buck will walk on. Forget about where the trails are located. Every "dead zone" around your stand reduces your odds for success.

You can't shoot what you can't see. Taking the time to cut that one extra lane might mean a filled tag instead of frustration.

73

A MATTER OF TIME AND ATTITUDE

When I'm sitting on stand I can mentally picture the meter slowly turning. In the morning it might read 75 percent. At noon maybe it's 76 percent. By the time I climb down it's 78 percent. Eventually it's going to reach 100 percent, and my time will come to draw my bow on another big one. The more attention to detail you pay, the faster the meter turns, but it will happen eventually. It has to. Time on stand is the practical part of hunting strategy. It is where the rubber meets the road. Without time on stand, everything else in this chapter is worthless philosophy. Each minute you hunt brings you one minute closer to tagging the buck of your dreams.

———————

"Every 'dead zone' around your stand
reduces your odds for success."

———————

There is more to persistence than just hunting every day. You have to do your best to be in each stand when it is most likely to produce action. You can accomplish this by having plenty of stands to choose from and then spot-checking them occasionally to find out which ones are the hottest. By slipping carefully in and checking the sign in the general area of each stand, you can tell when the deer are really using the location. I look for large tracks much the same way a bear guide studies the ground to identify his best baits for producing bulky bruins. By looking first in fringe areas, such as road crossings and field edges, you don't run the risk of messing up a sensitive hunting area before you even get a chance to hunt it.

Hunting all day is a sure way to increase your stand time and your odds, but it can be an incredible battle with boredom. I can only do it for a few days in a row, so I only hammer it during the peak of the rut. Bucks will move all day at these times, and success can come at any moment. Every minute is important. Don't ever forget that. (More on "Hunting All Day" in Chapter 5.)

I used a lot of missed opportunities to illustrate my points in this story. It is easier to learn valuable lessons from painful experiences than from pleasant ones. Every time a big buck gets away, there's usually a lesson to be learned. I've had more than my share of these sessions, and each time the answer has come down to laziness in one of the areas I discussed in this story. Remember, everything you do, or don't do, will affect your odds for success.

The Little Things

The list of hunters whose dreams have been shattered by small equipment malfunctions is long and particularly bitter. I know a

guy who had a bona fide Boone and Crockett Club buck at 15 yards. His treestand squeaked as he shifted his weight while drawing his bow. The buck bolted. I saw it on video.

Another giant B&C trophy was coming to rattling when the hunter's stand creaked as he shifted his weight that cold, still morning. At 60 yards the buck turned tail. Squeaky treestands have saved many a deer. Put your stand to the test before the season and fix any noisemakers. Paying attention to every aspect of your equipment and not taking anything for granted will increase your odds for success.

Can you increase your odds by shortening the range at which a deer can scent you? You bet you can! Is it worth the extra effort? You tell me. Dressing in the field helps you avoid household odors that could alert deer. Store your outerwear and boots in a sealed container that stays in the truck. Playing the odds comes down to just these types of decisions. Hunters who are willing to put out the effort to address every detail of the hunt are the ones who seem to be "lucky" enough to bag big bucks on a regular basis.

BEFORE THE LEAVES FALL

by Charles J. Alsheimer

If temperatures rise, water can pull in deer during daylight hours. Generally, deer travel shorter distances in early autumn than they will as the rut nears.

*T*he rut drives whitetail hunters. For the avid deer hunter, the magic of November (or whenever breeding takes place) inspires dreams of hunting rutting bucks. It's truly a time all deer hunters yearn for. But as grand as that time is, hunting during the time just prior to the rut—before the leaves fall (what others call the pre-rut)—can be as productive as the rut.

Historically, the whitetail's pre-rut has generated limited interest among deer hunters. Many view it as nothing more than a warm-up stage, a time to see what's in the woods, a time to start thinking about big bucks and the opportunities of November. But with each passing year, more and more hunters realize that whitetails often provide more and better opportunities in late October before the leaves fall from the trees.

EARLY AUTUMN BEHAVIOR

For the most part, whitetails are very secretive creatures during September and early October. As September eases into October, the whitetail's thick winter coat grows in. This heavier fur, coupled with autumn's warm days, causes whitetails to be less active during daylight hours. As a result, they move at either edge of day and feed under the protection of night.

During this time period, I've observed a phenomenon that I call "staging." Prior to a buck peeling its velvet, sightings are fairly consistent. However, once they've shed their velvet, bucks—especially dominant bucks—go into hiding.

"Heavier fur, coupled with autumn's warm days, causes whitetails to be less active during daylight hours."

Throughout much of their range, they seem to curtail their activity drastically during late September and October. It's almost like they are resting up for the rigors of November's rut when they'll be continually on the move. Does, on the other hand, seem to continue their normal movement patterns. As a result, with doe sightings high and buck sightings low, hunting the pre-rut period can be very frustrating.

However, there is a bright side to hunting whitetails early. During this time, the bucks are in bachelor groups and it's not uncommon to find several together. I've seen as many as seven bucks walk by my stand during an early-season sit. That is definitely a plus when hunting this time of year. A key to remember is that once the rut arrives, group behavior is over.

"Once they've shed their velvet, bucks—especially dominant bucks—go into hiding."

OFF-SEASON SCOUTING

Scouting during late winter and spring allows me to analyze what took place the preceding season as well as to learn about the bucks that survived. I'm also able to scout bedding areas actively to learn more about deer habits. One of the key aspects of scouting the bedding area in late winter is that it eliminates pressuring a buck. This, along with locating the preceding fall's food source, helps determine how to hunt a given buck or area come early fall. Remember—those food sources are your ticket to success during the pre-rut period.

Research has shown that it's not uncommon for bucks to increase their body weight by 25 percent during the months of September and October. Knowing this, I scout for the whitetail's main food source during late August and early September, staying out of the bedding areas I located the previous winter and spring.

Deer activity during late September and early October is at a low ebb because of the factors already mentioned. Bucks, particularly mature bucks, travel little during this time. Rather, they are content to lie low and cover little ground. This behavior makes them far more predictable during this time than during the rut. Before the leaves fall, bucks instinctively seem to get ready for the rut and all the activity associated with it. As a result, they crave food—lots of it.

Food preference varies across the country, but where I live, in western New York, old apple orchards, stands of oak, beechnuts, corn, alfalfa and fall-planted grain fields offer distinct hotspots for pre-rut whitetails. Field crops and apples are easy to locate, but mast can be a different story. If there is a good acorn crop, some acorns will start falling in late August. Also, I use a good pair of binoculars to scan the tree-tops looking for acorns and beechnuts.

However, not every stand of oaks or every apple orchard is a hotspot. Don't expect to ambush a whitetail coming to feed during the pre-rut unless there is ample cover and available escape routes. If the necessities aren't there, these food sources will only be visited during the night.

THE APPLE CONNECTION

Probably more pre-rut bucks have been killed in or near apple orchards than any other place. During the early-autumn months, deer habitat is in a state of change, and much plant life is stalky and not to a deer's liking. Consequently, when apples start falling, whitetails gravitate to them. Over the years, I've surprised more than one buck as he came to gorge on apples.

On occasion, I erect a portable stand in the orchard if a given tree offers good possibilities. However, if many trees in the area are bearing apples, my strategy changes. Where many bearing trees are present, I locate my stand where the deer must pass to get to the orchard. I prefer this type of ambush because once deer get into an orchard, it is nearly impossible to determine which way they will go. Usually a whitetail will gravitate to whichever tree has the most apples under it on a given day. Normally there will be multiple trails leading into the orchard where a stand can be erected.

Feed is especially critical early in the season as whitetails bulk up. Soft mast, most notably apples, is difficult to beat for bucks.

Mast areas will attract deer and see rutting activity as autumn progresses.

HUNTING MAST

If the bedding area around a food source is not well defined, deer will come to feed from literally any direction. If this is the case, I'll erect my stand where I find the most sign—heavy mast on the ground and concentrations of droppings—and move my stand accordingly if needed.

When hunting in mast areas, I also attempt to find a whitetail signpost—a tree that is rubbed year after year. Usually, if mast is present, the signpost and area around it will become more and more active as the rut approaches. Such locations are excellent places for hunting and are frequently visited by several bucks during the course of the season.

AGRICULTURAL AREAS

Clover, alfalfa and rye or wheat fields can also be very productive hunting locations before the leaves fall. Whitetails sense the nutritional value of a particular food and prefer clover and alfalfa when it is present.

Unfortunately, hunting around such fields presents problems because deer tend to visit them only under the cover of darkness; however, if the area is made up of small fields with adequate cover, deer will work them the last hour of the day and very early in the morning. But evening hunts will generally be the more productive.

Erecting treestands along well-used trails leading to the field can provide a good deal of action. In most cases, it is important to hang the stand at least 15 feet high and a minimum of 50 yards inside the cover in order to get action during legal shooting light. If you're not seeing deer with this type of setup, you'll have to locate closer to the bedding area.

Trail hunting in and around food sources is at its best during this early season. When I'm hunting a trail, I like to be at least 15 yards off the trail. Being too close to the deer run creates a host of problems, the greatest being a deer smelling or seeing you before he arrives in range. Also, avoid placing a stand on a curve in the trail where deer can spot you when they come around it.

In order to continue hunting a given area when the wind shifts, I secure two stand locations, one upwind and one downwind of where I think a buck will appear. Because food sources continually change, I'm a big fan of portable treestands. Portables allow for optimum movement within an area without disrupting a buck's habits. Where legal and possible, you should prepare shooting lanes from your stand. After all, it does no good to make all the preparations for a hunt and not be able to shoot when a buck shows up.

DON'T OVER-HUNT

When hunting pre-rut bucks, I try to locate several good food sources to make sure that I don't over-hunt a location. Over-hunting an area is one of the biggest mistakes hunters make. Regardless of how hot an area might be, don't over-hunt it. I make it a point never to spend more than three consecutive sits in a given area. If a stand area is hunted

Stay out all day, but don't over-hunt any one location.

every day during the pre-rut, bucks will simply change their patterns and either leave the area or become nocturnal.

If the food source holds, the location becomes better and better as September fades into October because bucks begin making scrapes. When these first scrapes are actively worked, a buck's territory is smaller than it will become in late October. As a result, bucks are more predictable in hitting these scrapes again. Generally, if thick cover presents itself in areas of heavy oak mast or in apple orchards, bucks will work scrapes during daylight hours.

RUT INDICATORS

If a scrape is located in an active feeding area, check the condition of the overhanging licking branch to determine its use. Examining the size of tracks in the scrape will also reveal a lot about the size of bucks using a particular area. Research has shown that if the tracks exceed $2\frac{1}{4}$ inches in width, the animal will weigh more than 175 pounds. If this is the case, it's probably a buck two-and-a-half years of age or older. Often, these early scrapes will turn into primary scrapes (where much of the breeding is done) when the peak of the rut hits in November.

CALLING AND RATTLING IN THE PRE-RUT

Because whitetails are very social creatures, I rely heavily on calling during the pre-rut. Bucks, particularly yearlings, are very receptive to doe bleats and buck grunts. If I spot a buck that doesn't appear to be coming my way, I'll make two or three doe bleats or young buck grunts. Often this is all it takes to bring a buck in close. If it's a yearling buck, I will not use a low guttural grunt (characteristic of a mature buck), because there is a high probability that the sound will spook it. However, I'll use the low guttural grunt if the buck is mature. The key is to have a grunt tube that allows you to make several different vocalizations.

Rattling can work, and often does, for early-season hunters. But unlike the rut, when I rattle loudly and aggressively, my pre-rut rattling technique consists of trying to create the sound of two bucks sparring. As a result, I just tickle the antler tines together for five to 10 minutes in an attempt to bring a curious buck to my stand.

THE WEATHER CONNECTION

Learning to be a weather watcher will prove to be as important in the pre-rut as it is to know what the deer are eating. Over the years I've become an ardent weather watcher because of what I know it does to a whitetail's feeding habits. The subject of weather could fill volumes, but basically whitetails are more active during irregular weather patterns. A rapidly falling barometer usually puts whitetails in a feeding frenzy. Therefore, just prior to a storm's arrival will be an excellent time to be overlooking an apple orchard

It's simple but true: Good food sources attract whitetails and hold them in the vicinity.

or stand of oaks. Whitetails will also increase their feeding activity after a low-pressure system moves from an area and a high-pressure pattern returns. Once the low-pressure system moves on and the barometer rises, deer might feed heavily for three or four days to catch up on the "meals" they missed because of the inclement weather.

Perhaps the greatest benefit of hunting pre-rut whitetails is being able to hunt in the mild weather. There is nothing more enjoyable than hunting whitetails when the weather is comfortable. True, deer might not move as much as when cold weather arrives, but it's a special experience to be in a treestand as the last rays of sunlight fade from the forest. It's a time not only to reflect but to anticipate what each new day brings as the calendar creeps toward the rut. And that's another beauty of being out there before the leaves fall.

THE LOW-IMPACT APPROACH

by Bill Winke

The farmer's soft, easy words rocked me like a stiff right hook to the jaw. "I just walked into the woods and sat down and there he was," Charlie said. My friend had decided to do a little fall turkey hunting, one of his favorite pastimes. He had gone up on "the knob," on a part of his farm near a stand where I'd spent many fruitless hours. He proceeded to pick a stump and to pull out his call.

"Well, a little before sunset I saw this smaller buck come out of the cornfield a short distance away. He was following a doe. A few minutes later I got ready to leave. I just happened to look over my shoulder and there stood the most beautiful buck you can imagine. His rack was tall and wide. I suppose if I'd had a bow I could have shot him right there."

"Yeah, I saw him up there from the road through binoculars a couple days ago," I replied. "He was massive with a long drop tine off his left beam." Then, from my lofty perch of false assurance, I elaborated on the size of the drop-tine buck, how his typical frame would have scored in the 150s or 160s and how I had tried to sneak in front of him to no avail. Charlie smiled politely. "Yeah, I know which one you're talking about," he said. "That drop-tine buck was the smaller one that was followin' the doe. The other one was huge."

WHAM! My eyes rolled back and my knees started to buckle from the impact of the vicious blow. I looked down at my boot toe as I kicked weakly at the big tire on Charlie's combine. I could only shake my head in bewilderment. How many times had I heard this story? It seemed that the two weeks I had just spent busting my hump had been a total waste of time. All I had to do was "walk into the woods and pick a stump."

SEEING THE PATTERN

Think back on all the stories you've heard from squirrel hunters, turkey hunters or beginners involving a close encounter with a truly huge buck. The odds seem staggering against such an occurrence, yet it happens with agonizing regularity. I remember the guy who "accidentally" wandered into one of my best hunting areas in the predawn darkness. With no more knowledge of the area than the fact that he had found a climbable tree, he erected his stand in time to watch

Sure, it's important to scout. But spending too much time and leaving too much scent near prospective stand sites can affect deer movements in the immediate area. A hit-and-run approach catches deer off guard.

31 deer pass in the course of a couple hours. Three were bucks that would have qualified for the Pope and Young Club's bowhunting record book. One was the huge 10-pointer that I'd hunted the previous week without ever seeing him. Give me a break! Is this sport just pure luck?

What do all these occurrences have in common? What is there about "beginner's luck" that makes it such a good strategy for monster bucks? What could I learn from these seemingly accidental successes that could be applied to improve my chances for a really outstanding buck? That's the question I wrestled with as I drove the quarter-mile down Charlie's driveway, and for days afterward.

HUMAN SCENT OVERDOSE

What I took from that day has affected the way I've hunted trophy bucks every season since. I finally realized that beginners are the ultimate low-impact hunters. What could offer less warning than simply walking into the woods and choosing a spot that "just felt good?" No scouting. No scent left from a previous trip. Nothing to give an ultra-suspicious buck notice that something's up. Before I tell you how I applied this knowledge, we first need to look at important factor in balancing our impact: human ground scent.

I was heading to a great stand, maybe my best that year. I had seen some dandy bucks from it in past seasons, and I was looking forward to a repeat performance. Fifteen yards from the stand, I had to cross a well-used deer trail that lay between the withered yellow cornstalks I had just sneaked through and the field's brushy perimeter. I decided to jump across the deer trail just to make sure I wouldn't leave any scent within three feet of it.

The first group of does and fawns came past 45 minutes later. The lead doe hit my crossing and immediately locked up. What could she possibly be smelling? The wind was blowing straight from her to me; I had worn knee-high rubber boots, washed my clothes in unscented soap, showered before the hunt, sprayed scent eliminator on my pants legs, even danced a jig in a "cow pie" before entering the field. Finally, without flagging, blowing or otherwise signaling her alarm, the doe simply reversed course and slipped quietly into the standing corn, taking the rest of the herd with her. "Dang! What a spooky doe," I thought to myself. "I haven't been in this area for a whole year!"

A half hour later another good-sized group of does and fawns waltzed up the trail. (Where were all the bucks on this perfect November morning?) As I sat petrified in my tree, their carefree movements immediately changed to visible tension as the whole herd stumbled into the leader who again had frozen on point at my trail crossing. The performance of the first group was repeated, and these deer also faded into the corn.

The final blow came when a single yearling doe came walking up the trail with her head held high and simply turned inside out when she hit my entry trail. First, she dashed one direction and then the other. She really wanted to cross my path but apparently feared for her very life should she do so. Finally, gathering all her speed and courage, she sprang high in the air, completely clearing the area containing my scent before racing madly into the nearby woods. That left me sick and empty, as if I had just witnessed a traffic accident. I knew I could never beat a deer's nose, no matter how hard I tried. Seeing how they reacted left little doubt that I was messing up my stands every time I hunted them. And so are you! It was the most depressing day I had ever spent in a treestand, but it was also the most enlightening. I obviously needed to give more thought to the subject of managing human ground scent.

As you leave the woods, your airborne scent leaves with you. Ground scent, on the other hand, remains for days in some cases, alerting every deer that runs across it, long after we go home. I've had thousands of opportunities to watch deer react to ground scent. In certain parts of the country, especially in dry climes and in areas with high deer densities, they seem to pay it little mind. Young deer will let you get by with more, sniffing the ground and brush a few times before going on about their business. And there are areas where people are more common in the woods, causing deer to become somewhat desensitized. Yet, even under the best of conditions, I've never seen a mature buck (or doe, for that matter) walk past my scent trail without getting nervous and taking some form of evasive action as a result. By now you should see that leftover human scent plays a major role in determining your trophy success rate.

FIRST CHANCE IS YOUR BEST

Have you ever wondered why the first time you sit on a stand is usually the best time? Residual ground scent is one of the main reasons, especially if the stand is located right in an area with high deer activity. Each time you hunt the stand, you leave more scent and educate more deer (in a number of different ways) until the spot becomes deer hunting's version of a ghost town.

If you try to hunt an area more than once or twice, chances are that any resident mature buck knows he is being hunted long before you get a crack at him. The buck only needs to make one nocturnal trip across your trail to know that his previously safe, undisturbed haven of refuge has been invaded by a human. In many cases he'll simply move on or use the area only after he has carefully checked it out from downwind. Either way, you lose. Cruising bucks might still pass through the area, but once all the mature does have wised up and changed their behavior, even cruisers are unlikely visitors.

There are other forms of human impact besides ground scent. Deer can see you in the stand or walking to and from it; or if the wind swirls or shifts slightly, they will smell you. All of these events spell trouble, especially when they occur more than once.

Every discussion on the subject of human impact finds its way back to a central issue: Your best chance to take a trophy buck is the first time you venture into his domain. This being true, why not make every time on stand a first time? How is that possible? Let's go back to the story I started earlier.

After leaving my friend Charlie's farm those many years ago, I was struck by the fact that I needed a different approach to trophy hunting. I needed a strategy that allowed me to take advantage of the strengths of the beginner. Then it occurred to me: I too would just walk into a spot that I had not been to for months, or maybe ever. I'd simply pick a spot that felt good, put up a stand and start hunting. I somehow knew it would work, and two days later I found out.

TESTING THE THEORY

I hadn't seen a thing that morning even though it was dead calm and frosty with the rut in full swing. By the time I left my stand I had already made up my mind that my afternoon hunt was going to be in a completely fresh area. As soon as I got home I pulled out my aerial photos looking for a place I knew had deer but had not been hunted (or even scouted) that season. I found what I was looking for on a farm that I had been given permission to hunt only a month earlier.

From the photo, I could see a narrow draw that connected several fingers of brush and trees with a large block of timber. It seemed the perfect spot to ambush a cruising buck. As closely as possible, I picked my post from the photo. Shortly after noon, I sneaked directly to the spot with my stand on my back.

While standing in one place, I could see a spot where two good trails came together on my side (the downwind side) of the draw. I chose a tree that would allow me to cover both trails, as well as any random movement down through the bottom of the draw. It just felt good! Using tree steps, I quickly climbed the tree, then slipped the pin-mounted stand off my back and quietly into place. I climbed on, trimmed a couple of limbs and pulled up my bow. I was hunting.

Just before sunset a nice 10-pointer came into view. Cutting across the draw, he began following one of the trails right toward me. Head down, he was scent checking for does as he worked my way at a steady pace. Broadside, at a range of only 12 yards, I couldn't miss. In that one successful afternoon, my lifelong hunting strategy took a 90-degree turn.

BECOMING VERSATILE

By putting up a stand and hunting it immediately, rather than the next day or the next week, we give ourselves the best possible chance of catching hunter-wise bucks using normal, undisturbed patterns. Think of it as making your own beginner's luck! You need to be able to do three things really well to make this approach work for you.

Be quiet and stealthy. First and foremost, you need to be able to carry a stand into the woods and put it up quickly and quietly. There are any number of ways to accomplish this. I

Portable stands are the favored treestand flavor for low-impact hunting. Find a model that you can hang quickly, quietly and safely.

still prefer screw-in tree steps for my own hunting due to their versatility, but I realize the physical exertion that is required to climb a tree in this manner is not for everyone. Sectional climbing ladders are versatile and have become very popular in recent years. You might want to check them out.

The stand you choose must go up quietly. I prefer lightweight aluminum stands for this type of hunting because they are easier to handle quietly than are heavy stands. Fixed-position stands are the best overall choice because you're not always going to find a tree that is straight enough to use a climbing stand. You can usually find a tree that will allow you to hang a chain-on, strap-on or pin-mounted stand. My personal preference for this type of hunting are the pin-mounted styles.

Improvise. You also need to be good at flying by the seat of your pants. In some cases, you'll be choosing hunting spots without the benefit of any type of scouting. Fortunately, there are enough resources available, such as tracks on road crossings and field edges, aerial photos, topo maps and conversations with landowners and local residents, that you can pull this off with reasonable effectiveness. The better you become at using these resources, especially the aerial photos, the better will be your stand choices.

I'm about as dependent upon aerial photos as I am upon my bow or my treestand. Sitting at home, I can "walk" a property without exposing a single deer to my scent. All the terrain and cover that serve to funnel deer are right there in black and white. I can tell where the bedding ridges are, where the deer are most likely to feed, where the heaviest cover is (darkest areas on the photos) and where the travel routes connecting all this good stuff are located. Aerial photos are most easily obtained through the county soil conservation office in the county seat where you hunt.

Gain hunting access. Finally, you need to be good at gaining access to hunting areas. Since you will be moving around often with this style of hunting, you'll need more ground to hunt. I realize that in some parts of the country this is a problem. Do the best you can. If you can get access to a couple of good areas, your options really open up.

LOW-IMPACT SCOUTING

Whenever possible, spend some time scouting *after* the season—when your presence won't hurt your chances for success later, in order to learn all you need to know. While you're at it, pick several likely stand sites. You might even choose to put a couple of stands up at this time. You're going to need some morning stands anyway, as it is nearly impossible to pick a tree and put up a stand in the darkness of predawn. You'll also run across some spots that are prime candidates for this low-impact hunting method. Jot them down in a notebook and come back during the season with a stand on your back.

PRACTICE MAKES PERFECT

One of the goals in low-impact hunting is to keep ground scent to a minimum so that approaching deer won't detect it before they get to you. The drawback to hit-and-run stand hunting is that you don't have the luxury of doing a bunch of on-the-ground scouting. As a result, you're going to miss the perfect stand site from time to time. It can be frustrating to see big bucks passing out of range, but any hunt is successful when you see such animals in the first place. Besides, you'll get better at this as you go along and you'll pull everything together often enough. You might need to choose a tree that is more open than you normally would select, just so there will be plenty of clear shooting lanes. It is better to take small chances with concealment than to risk not getting a shot at a nice buck.

This is definitely a demanding hunting style, both mentally and physically. But I can't think of a better way to lower your impact. The harder you work at it, the better you'll do. When I started hunting this way, the number of big bucks I saw immediately increased. Now it's about the only way I hunt. And in my opinion, it's the deadliest possible strategy for the serious trophy hunter.

A midday break and a look at the topo map might give you a bright idea for catching a buck on a fresh piece of turf.

82

PLAYING THE WIND

by Judd Cooney

There should be no doubt in any serious whitetail hunter's mind about the importance wind plays in his success or failure. Wind, and its propensity for carrying the dreaded human scent to the super-sensitive nostrils of a wary whitetail, is probably responsible for more than 90 percent of the unsuccessful encounters between hunter and deer. Even though many hunters are aware of this important aspect of their whitetail hunting ventures, most don't fully understand the idiosyncrasies of the wind and air currents that can wreak havoc with their chances. They don't know how to use the wind to their advantage or simply don't give a damn, and they go on their way in ignorant bliss.

Many hunters are vaguely aware of wind patterns in hilly country where the wind rises as the sun comes up and falls down the slope as the sun sets. If only dealing with wind currents were that simple we would all be a lot more successful. Add a few gullies on the slope, thickets of trees, rock ledges or open parks and you have wind patterns, currents, updrafts, downdrafts, swirls and counter-currents that can drive you nuts and defeat even the best-laid hunting plans.

Ever wonder why deer—especially mature bucks—like to travel below the ridges and above the bottoms of the draws? Obviously the visibility is better and they are not being skylined on the top of the ridge, but the main reason is the simple fact that the wind currents on the sides of the slopes are far more stable and predictable, and the deer can use them with much more confidence to detect danger from above or below. The breezes on the top of a ridge and in the valley or gully bottoms are as unpredictable for deer as they are for hunters, so the deer travel where they can depend on stable air currents.

In flat country, wind currents are much more predictable but can still give you fits—unless you take some time to study their patterns and learn all you can about them as they apply to your particular hunting area. Such terrain features as dark-colored plowed or lush green fields that absorb more heat during the day than the surrounding woods can cause updrafts of warm air as the evening cools. This could mean that a hunter in a treestand at the edge of the field would be undetectable to any deer along the edge or in the field while a hunter

100 yards back in the woods might have his scent swirling down around his stand and spooking every deer within a 50-yard radius. A steady breeze, hitting a brushy stream bank or other natural obstacle in its path, might be deflected high enough on the far side of the obstacle to carry a hunter's scent far above the nose of any approaching whitetail, provided you stay within the area affected by the updraft. A lot can be learned about air movement when it encounters obstacles by taking the time to study water currents in a stream full of logs or rocks. Most of the time you can gain a decided advantage by knowing just how wind currents operate and by studying them in your hunting area.

HOW TO WORK THE WIND

I would rather put my faith in the wind and make it work for me rather than against me. If you have the wind currents, drafts, breezes or thermals working in your favor, you are going to get closer to whitetails more often. But there will still be occasions when Mother Nature throws you a split-second downdraft, updraft or thermal swirl that will ruin your day.

Test the air currents continually while you're hunting.

"Wind ... is probably responsible for more than 90 percent of the unsuccessful encounters between hunter and deer."

The most valuable hunting tool that I have found for winning the war of wind is a simple but effective squeeze bottle full of talcum powder. Many whitetail hunters tie a piece of dental floss or feather to their bow or gun and use it to determine wind currents. These tactics are far better than simply ignoring the wind as most unsuccessful deer hunters do, but a feather or floss falls far short of being as effective as a powder bottle.

There is always air movement! With a powder bottle you can pick up the most subtle breeze, updraft, downdraft or almost undetectable convection current or thermal drift.

Constant use of a powder bottle during your scouting trips—while you are walking through your hunting area or sitting in a treestand—will continually upgrade your knowledge of the wind characteristics in your hunting area and go a long way toward letting you avoid detection by a wary buck's sense of smell. Carry a scouting logbook and note the weather and wind conditions in your hunting area and around your stands during various times of the year; these entries will give you a ready reference for future use and might turn out to be your most important notes.

Being constantly aware of wind currents is more important to bowhunters than to gun hunters simply because of the "up-close-and-personal" distances involved. However, a gun hunter who doesn't pay attention to the wind is missing a sure step in becoming a better and more successful hunter. A bowhunter must avoid the deer's keen sense of smell at point-blank range where there is no distance factor to dilute or disperse the dreaded human scent. Any whitetail catching the slightest whiff of human scent at 30 yards or less is history for the waiting bowhunter. If the deer is a mature buck you can probably write that stand or particular area off for the rest of the season as far as that specific deer is concerned.

Many bowhunters take all the precautions in the book to kill or cover their odor. They shower, shave and wash their hair and clothes in scent-eliminating soaps and solutions. They spray and splash all sorts of concoctions on themselves and anything else that will hold still, to eliminate or cover the human odor—all in hopes that they can fool a deer's nose

Whitetails prefer to travel near ridgetops where wind currents are more reliable. Hunting the bottom often results in failure because of swirling breezes.

into thinking they don't exist. These precautions are all fine and good when combined with scent-free, clean outer clothing and footwear, and taking measures to leave as little scent as possible on trails, bushes, fences, trees and such in your hunting area and near a stand location. All this preparation might dilute the human scent enough to allow a deer to pass through the area without reaching the panic stage and help in allowing what scent there is to dissipate more rapidly. I don't personally believe that there is anything on the market at this point that will keep a hunter completely scent-free under most hunting conditions, but you have to try!

GET THE DRIFT

The best way to make these precautions work for your benefit most of the time is to make the wind work for you *all* the time! A powder bottle is the tool that can make this possible. You can use a powder bottle to check the wind from a number of different locations around a proposed stand location to determine a site where the wind is the least likely to betray your presence. There are times when simply moving your treestand a few trees one way or the other or placing your stand a few feet higher in the tree will get you into an entirely different wind current flow and totally eliminate the chances of a deer smelling you. Studying the drift of the talcum powder will often easily pinpoint such a location for you. You might have located a super deer funnel that could be hunted all day if it wasn't for the wind changing. By interpreting the wind drift at the different times of day with your powder bottle you can erect several stands to cover the area regardless of the wind conditions. When you are actually hunting such an area, use your powder bottle periodically another area, the outfitter and his wife returned to the field to put in a stand for me. Since there were no trees along the edge of the field that would hold a treestand, they improvised and dug and brushed up a shallow pit blind for me. That afternoon the outfitter's wife dropped me at the blind, and I settled down for the wait. The afternoon was hot, and the stiff breeze was quartering across my front, eliminating any chance of deer winding me approaching the field on the well-used trail in the corner of the pocket.

Then some clouds bunched up over me and let loose with a torrential downpour for 15 minutes. As the sun lowered and the air cooled, the breeze died, but the talcum from my trusty powder bottle told me that there was an almost imperceptible current of air drifting directly across the field in front of me. No problem!

Bucks continually test the wind whether it's raining or the sun is shining, meaning you should be testing for wind shifts as well.

"Two fine bucks emerged from the corner of the bush and began feeding on an angle toward me."

As the evening progressed and the sun settled behind a cloud bank, several does moved out of the brush into the field and began feeding voraciously on the lush green wheat. Now I had a problem! One of the does was feeding my way about 10 yards from the edge of the brush line. If she got opposite me there was little doubt that she was going to be inundated by my cloud of scent drifting slowly across the field. To make matters worse, two fine bucks, both in the 140-inch category, emerged from the corner of the bush and began feeding on an angle toward me.

to check the wind. If the wind switches unexpectedly, the powder will tell you, and it's a simple matter to climb down and carefully move to one of the other stands. Much better than being detected and blowing the whole setup.

SIGNIFICANT SHIFTS

Under hunting conditions, a drifting cloud of talcum just might alert you to a wind change that could make a difference in where you take a shot. Several years ago I was bowhunting in Alberta, Canada, with an outfitter and not having much success. His wife had been scouting a winter wheat field one evening and spotted two record-class bucks and several does feeding in a small pocket adjacent to a section of heavy bush. The next morning while I was hunting

I eased my bow into shooting position and again tested the wind with a thin stream of talcum powder. The current was holding steady as I watched the doe and bucks moving closer. The doe was now less than 15 yards from me while the bucks were still 45 yards out. Fortunately, the doe found an extra-special clump of sedge to munch for a few extra seconds and gave the bucks a chance to cut the distance to 40 yards. When the doe started moving again, I tensed for the shot. She was less than 10 yards from my blind and probably only five yards from the edge of my scent stream when I centered my concentration on the larger buck, drew and

Beating Human Scent

Any hunter who's had a deer "blow" or "snort," signaling other deer of danger, knows how frustrating that situation is. There's nothing worse than having high hopes dashed by a doe that catches a whiff of your human scent. Sure, you can play the wind to your advantage when choosing stands, but deer don't always appear where you expect them to.

So it's wise to keep human scent to a minimum. Most veteran hunters agree that you can never totally eliminate human scent, but you can drastically reduce the odor that might alert a deer to your presence. Here's how:

First, make sure that your hunting clothes are washed regularly in scent-eliminating, scent-free detergent like that offered by many of the same companies that produce deer scent. Between hunts, store your clothing in a sealed plastic container—preferably somewhere outside where it is least likely to absorb household odors.

If at all possible, shower before you head out to hunt. Use a scent-free soap and shampoo. (Again, this stuff is available from companies like Robinson Labs and Wildlife Research Center.) From there, use a scent-free antiperspirant.

When you get to your hunting area, spray yourself down with a human scent-eliminating spray like those available from the companies listed above. And, of course, knee-high rubber boots are best during moderate temperatures since the rubber won't hold foreign odors.

To top it off, consider investing in a Scent-Lok suit with activated charcoal. A similar suit from Robinson Labs that features the company's ScentBlocker system also does a good job capturing any human odor that might still be present. These suits include top, bottom, hood and gloves to cover you completely. Wait till you get out of the truck at your hunting area to take the Scent-Lok suit from its storage bag and put it on. Ideally, these suits, which now come in camo patterns, are worn as the outermost layer, thereby capturing any scent on the under layers. However, if you wear the suit as an intermediate layer, be sure to use the scent-killing sprays on your outerwear. If you're going to be hunting all day, it's wise to carry

some scent-killing spray with you to re-apply when you move stands or during midday.

Trying to beat a whitetail's nose is hard work and requires attention to detail. You ought to pay attention to the wind, but you can't always trust it entirely. If these steps give you that extra second you need to kill a mature buck, it will be worth your time and effort.

—Gregg Gutschow

released. He had been a bit farther than I preferred, but the arrow was right on, and he was down for the count within 100 yards. At my shot, the doe exploded into action and headed back into the brush. If I hadn't been using a powder bottle, there was a very good chance that I would have unknowingly let the doe move into my scent stream and blow the whole show as I waited for the bucks to move within 25 yards or less. My trusty, tell-all powder bottle has saved the day for me on a number of similar occasions with whitetails, elk, pronghorns and bears. A cloud of talcum powder can also let you know when your chances of success in hunting a certain stand are zero and you had better call it quits before you ruin a good stand.

MORE POWDER POWER

One fall I was bowhunting from a morning stand that overlooked a major trail leading to a couple of food plots. The early morning weather was cool with heavily overcast skies and the likelihood of rain. The subtle breeze drifting through the woods in my favor made detection by any deer approaching from the food plot or the timbered slopes unlikely. Just as it was getting light enough to shoot, the skies opened up in a cold shower that cooled everything down considerably. I had anticipated a wet hunt and had my rain gear on and the tree-stand umbrella in place. I figured that with a cool, damp morning and the rut in progress there was a good chance that deer would be moving all morning and a good buck might just check the area around the food plot for scent of a doe in estrus.

Five minutes after the shower, the breeze died completely —well, almost! The cloud of talcum emitted from my plastic bottle settled around the base of the tree under my stand like an ever-expanding mushroom. I had no doubt that the longer I stayed put, the larger the cloud of scent would become—just hanging there to alert any and all approaching deer to my presence. The odds of ruining this stand for future hunting were far better than the chances of my getting a shot at a good buck, so I simply packed up and eased out of the area to wait for a morning when the air currents were in my favor.

A powder bottle is a deadly accessory for still-hunting and stalking also. There are times when you can stalk a deer or likely bedding area from the upwind side if you know exactly what the wind and air currents are doing. Oftentimes, all you have to do to keep your scent out of a likely place is to move slightly off to one side, just enough to let your scent be carried past the patch of cover and not into it. By periodically monitoring the wind with your powder bottle, you can almost always hunt with the breeze in your favor and greatly increase your chances of success.

"By periodically monitoring the wind with your powder bottle, you can almost always hunt with the breeze in your favor and greatly increase your chances of success."

I carry squeeze bottles of talcum in all my packs, camera bag, bow and gun kits, glove compartments of my vehicles and even one in my shaving kit, just in case. There are a lot of things I might leave behind when I go scouting or hunting, but you can bet your deer rifle that one of them isn't going to be my "windicator" powder bottle.

TREESTAND TECHNIQUES

by Gene and Barry Wensel

A lot of skill goes into a properly placed portable stand, as we're hunting for the exact spot to take a deer before we actually hunt the deer itself.

Permanent treestands were very common up to two decades go, but today they have too many disadvantages as far as we're concerned. Not only are they an eyesore, but once deer discover their location, they defeat their own purpose. Plus, they announce your hunting spots to other hunters. Permanent stands use spikes or nails that are often left in the tree. They can raise hell with a chainsaw if the tree is ever cut down for lumber. After longer periods of time, nails or spikes eventually make most permanent stands unsafe, too. We've all found old permanent stands that have fallen down by themselves after a few years. As a tree grows, the nails are actually pulled right through the boards themselves.

Like most modern deer hunters, we use only portable treestands. Other than ladders, wedges and sling-type stands, most portables are either of the hang-on or self-climbing varieties. We much prefer hang-on types for several reasons. Most self-climbers (not all) are heavy, awkward rattle-traps that spook almost as many deer as they earn. Secondly, self-climbers are limited to use on straight trees with minimal limbs. If you own and use a self-climber and like it for where and how you hunt, more power to you, but for our money, hang-ons have a lot more advantages.

Quite a few hunters use homemade hang-ons, which we also suppose is fine as long as you're confident in the design and safety of your finished product. Considering dealer prices from larger stand manufacturers, you should be able to get quality affordable hang-on types. One other interesting point. We can't believe how many hard-core deer hunters own only one treestand. Buy and use as many as you can afford. There's no limit to what you might need. There are hundreds of designs commercially available. Good ones all have a few similar characteristics. Look for stability, ease of hanging, cost, silence, comfort and safety. Safety is absolutely the first thing to consider. Put the stand up two feet off the ground. Jump on it. Stand on the very edges of the platform. Try to tip it.

Sectional ladders require less work than screw-in type treesteps. They are also often easier to climb safely.

Rest on it sideways. Kick it. You'll know a good brand when you find it.

Because we spend an enormous amount of time on stand, one of the next things we look for is comfort. Pick one with a seat that is not only comfortable, but the right height for your leg length. Look for one that will distribute weight evenly between your butt and your legs. We also prefer a seat that will fold up flat against the tree, silently.

SETTING THE STANDS

We do a lot of the decision-making of exactly how a stand will be placed from ground level before we put it in the tree. Decide from ground level the direction the platform will face. If you use screw-in treesteps, you can often mentally put them in from the ground, counting how

many you'll need as you go along. Sometimes it's best to start off with a right foot, other times its best to begin with a left. When you remove a screw-in treestep, put a small twig in the hole to mark the spot so that it's easy to find next time in low-light conditions.

We made two very common mistakes for years that spooked untold numbers of deer at close range. When erecting a stand, one of us would often sit on the ground close to the tree to "help." Your hunting partner's body print or hand print on the ground will leave enough human odor to spook deer from close range for up to three days, depending on weather conditions.

The second thing that consistently spooked deer was putting metal treesteps into the tree with bare hands. Winding a set of metal steps into the tree with sweaty bare hands will leave enough scent to spook deer. Metal retains human odor. You won't see a good trapper setting traps with bare sweaty hands! Wear gloves.

For 25 or 30 years we used screw-in tree steps. Trial and error taught us that certain brands of steps were better for specific types of tree bark. As stated earlier, we hunt out of cottonwood trees a lot. Because the bark is very deep and defined, a collapsible step works much better placed in the low spots between bark ridges. Be aware that some bark is thicker than others. A step must be set into the meat of the tree, not just the bark.

Where we hunt, we often leave stands in the woods year-round. Unfortunately, long periods of time eventually rot the wood immediately around the thread part of a screw-in treestep. Never leave screw-in steps in a tree seasonally. In the past couple seasons, we've gone to hang-on ladders and/or climbing sticks. Either type hangs right onto the tree rather than screwing into it. Another positive feature of the ladders and sticks is that they mount six inches or so away from the tree trunk. With screw-in steps, your chest or stomach tends to push your body away from the tree, especially on big men. Use of a climbing stick or a hang-on ladder allows your body to flex toward the tree, giving much better control and balance.

As we get older, heavier and wiser, we tend to think more about safety. One careless slip can easily mess up a whole season or your entire life. Because we pre-hang most of our stands in spring, we aren't normally concerned about time, scent or noise in erecting stands.

Some readers might find this humorous, but we've finally come up with the optimum system for safety. (See diagram for details.) Working as a team, we first hang a chain-on platform about eye level from the ground. We hop up on it to hang a second platform, again at eye level. Climb up on this second platform, which is now about 10 feet off the ground. Use it to stand on while hanging your real hunting stand. Again at eye level, this final (third) platform will be 14 or 15 feet high. By utilizing the lower platforms, both hands are entirely free to work safely without having to hang on. When the top stand is seated, we then secure the ladders,

climbing stick or treesteps as we descend the tree, removing the bottom two platforms as we come down. Sure, it takes a bit longer and requires a little more effort in carrying in two extra platforms, but we've found it well worth the extra time and effort. For 20-plus years we hung on with a treestand in one hand, a chain in the other, trying to knee-pinch the tree while hanging on for dear life with everything up to and including our teeth. Without spare platforms to stand on while erecting a stand, heavy guys like us need about three more hands. Wisdom gained through trial and error has put all that behind us. We don't dread hanging stands at all now. In fact, we actually enjoy it, which makes this sport all the more fun.

SILENCING AND SOUPING UP STANDS

Most treestands eventually develop squeaks. A pair of small pliers is handy to tighten joints. So is a little plastic bottle of vegetable oil to lubricate any moving parts. Liquid vegetable oil in aerosol cans (like PAM) works well too. Elimination of any and all creaks is mandatory. It can mean the difference between a close shot and completely messing up an area.

Modification of our stands is standard procedure. Paint them with flat primer if they shine. Be sure to allow ample time for air drying before hunting.

For years we rubber dipped our chains. We can't say that it was worth the effort. Rubber

Why make hanging treestands an unsafe ordeal? Hang a stand from the ground. Hop up on it to hang a second stand. Then use that sturdy platform to hang a third stand, your hunting stand, at that optimal 14- or 15-foot height. Screw in tree steps as you descend and pull the bottom two stands. You're safe, in one piece and ready to hunt!

coating eventually frays and sometimes clogs the chain links that you need to use. The noise that rubber dipping eliminates is minimal since we pre-hang most of our stands anyway. If you carry your portable stand into the woods each time you use it, dipping the chain might be an option to look into. The rubber dip now available in spray cans works best. Some stands use ropes or belts rather than chain. They might be a little lighter to carry, but we prefer the bite of a good chain. A thief can cut a rope or belt with a pocket knife to steal your stand. Chains allow your stand to be padlocked onto the tree. Make your lock visible from the ground to discourage theft. Because we hunt out of some huge cottonwood trees here in the West, we use chain extensions regularly. One- or two-foot extensions added with a false link work well. Be sure to paint shiny new chain extensions.

A bowholder attached right to the stand itself can be very

handy, although we frequently use smaller clipped tree branches or various screw-in hooks to hang all sorts of gear. Being able to keep your hands in your pockets is a real advantage on long, cold days. Some might argue that a bow or gun holder causes unnecessary movement when game is sighted. But we find that shifting a gun or bow from hand to hand often results in a lot more movement. Get comfortable up there. We can't remember ever spooking an animal because we've had our bows hung up. As long as you know when and how to move, it becomes a minimal problem.

Always use a good haul-line to lift your gun, bow, arrows or any other equipment into your stand after you've climbed up and strapped yourself in. Use the same haul-line to lower gear before leaving. We prefer some sort of grilled platform on our stands. A see-through platform is one of the most underrated features of a good stand. From the ground, a stand with a solid platform catches attention of both deer and thief. Light, wind, rain and snow all pass through a grilled platform. They also provide better traction with ice or

---

"Get comfortable up there. As long as you know when and how to move, hanging your gun or bow becomes a minimal problem."

Permanent stands are eyesores, often dangerous and seldom productive over the long term. It doesn't take a whitetail long to realize that trouble lurks.

snow underfoot—especially if you wear air-bob soles on your hunting boots. We routinely stick a couple sprigs or boughs in the grid of the platform to help camouflage the stand itself.

One quick note for those of you who prefer adding carpet to treestand platforms. Use new carpet. Old carpet contains years of ground-in odor that, because of rain, eventually ends up around the base of our tree. When using carpet, attach it by the front edge of the stand only. This way, the carpet can be flipped forward while the stand is vacated so it won't accumulate snow when not in use. When getting new carpet for use on a stand platform, get the deep nap in some sort of camouflage or drab color.

DETAILING

Some hunters might consider us pretty fanatical about detailing and trimming. I've checked other people's tree-stands. On occasion, I'm tempted to challenge them to get off a shot in a normal fashion. There's a definite happy medium here too, as too much can be overkill. I remember once using a friend's stand with permission. The absolute only way he could have gotten off a shot with a bow would have been if he had used an extremely short-limbed bow held horizontally. It might have worked for a rifle hunter, but the stand was in an archery-only area.

When I climb into a stand, I mentally try to picture all feasible deer approach possibilities to determine what trimming is necessary. We divide hand saws into three types. Small folders are handy to carry in a fanny pack and are also useful in splitting pelvic bones or for quartering larger game. Look for the blade type where the teeth cut in both directions. I've never seen much need to carry a small chainsaw, but a medium buck saw with decent-sized teeth makes larger work a lot easier than trying to do the same job with a folding saw.

Years of experience has taught us that a pole pruner is one of the most valuable and necessary pieces of equipment for erecting a great stand. If you shop around, you can find a good-quality pole pruner for less than $50. One with a six-foot-long fiberglass extension pole that pulls out to 12 feet will allow you to reach more than 16 feet easily. Most brands have curved saw blades for ease in cutting, plus a good-sized pruner for snipping branches smaller than your thumb. Cutting shooting lanes without a pole pruner can be very frustrating. I remember for years searching the forest floor for long limbs, throwing whatever we found up at tiny twigs in hopes of clearing them. I've even had to put several screw-in treesteps into small trees in order to climb up to remove just one small branch in the way of a possible shot. With a pole pruner, those problems are all gone. We consider a pole pruner one of our most valuable tools for erecting a good treestand, yet few hunters use them.

For trimming smaller limbs and twigs around the stand itself or in the ground blind, nothing works as well as ratchet-cut hand pruners. It's a lightweight tool so we often carry one on our belt right next to our knife. I don't know how I got along without this tool for so many years. I know I use pruners a lot more than I do the knife riding on my belt right alongside. For branches up to the size of your thumb, pruners are much quicker, cleaner and quieter than any saw. Be sure to get the ratchet-cut variety, not just ordinary hand pruners. The ratchet-cut type makes a hard squeeze almost effortless. With ratchet-cut pruners, a child can cut thumb-sized branches with ease.

Try to keep trimming and lane cutting to a minimum. We find that the best way is to have a partner walk where you expect deer to come through as you stand in the tree (assuming you aren't hunting the same day that you erect the

A pole pruner can work wonders, helping you carve out good shooting lanes.

stand). Try to clip only one shooting lane in each direction. This should give you ample opportunity, yet won't appreciably alter cover.

One variable that many hunters don't take into consideration is the angle to hang a stand in order to get a shot off with least movement. Relate the stand platform as the face of the clock, with the front center of the stand being twelve o'clock. Because we're right-handed and prefer broadside shots, I want the animal somewhere around the nine or 10 o'clock position. For left-handed shooters, the angle would be more like two or three o'clock. A stand not positioned right might cause a bowhunter to hit his elbow against the tree while drawing.

All these little details might seem trivial to some, but they often make the difference between a dream buck and a nightmare.

BEDTIME WHITETAILS

by Gary Clancy

The old-timer looked me hard in the eyes, and I didn't much like what I saw. Contempt, disgust, exasperation—it was all there, easy to read in the watery blue eyes beneath the bill of his tattered wool cap. I didn't know what I had done wrong, but I knew that whatever it was, it was serious.

"Where you from, boy?" the old timer asked.

"Down south, a town called Albert Lea, sir," I choked out.

"Figured you weren't from around here. Most folks 'round here know better than to go stumbling right through a big buck's bedding area." He waited for me to say something, but I didn't have anything to say. Hell, I didn't have any idea what he was talking about.

"All day I've been sitting up there on the ridge in that little blowdown," he said, jabbing a mittened thumb in the direction of the ridge but never taking his eyes off mine. "I knew if I waited he would have to come out. The rut's on, you know. He doesn't have a choice. He had to move. It was just a matter of time. He would have, too, if you hadn't gone stomping right through his prime hidey-hole. I caught a glimpse of him sneaking out the side over there by that little alder run. Head low, tail tucked, slinking like a damn cat."

Again he paused. When he started again, I could see the meanness fade from his eyes. "You didn't know, did you?" he questioned, and before I could reply, he answered his own question. "Of course you didn't. It's not your fault, son, I didn't mean to be so hard on you. It's just that he was a big buck, a really big buck, and I've hunted him a long time and ... well, it doesn't matter now. But don't ever, no matter what, don't bother a buck in the place he beds. If you do, you won't ever see him there again, just like I won't ever see that buck near here again."

I stood there in the snow until he was out of sight, letting what he said sink in. It sunk in good. Twenty years passed, and I still believed what the old hunter in the northwoods had told me that day. In fact, the old man's words had been confirmed many times over those 20 years. Seemed that every article on deer hunting I read (and I read them all!) cautioned against disturbing a buck in his bedroom. One fall while hunting ruffed grouse, I got an inclination that maybe the old man had been wrong and that all of those writers had just been repeating each other.

My dog and I had hunted a lot that fall. One of the places we frequented was a large public hunting area dominated by mature timber, which grouse rarely use, but sprinkled with small parcels of new growth, which grouse dearly love. One of those bird-holding parcels was a long, narrow strip of baseball bat-thick aspen on the far western boundary of the property. Two of the four times we hunted that patch of aspens we put a very good buck out of his bed. The first time we jumped the buck, his focus was on my dog and I had a

very good look at him. The buck was an eight-pointer with average main beams, long tines, good mass and a 17-inch inside spread—a very good buck for public land. The second time we jumped him, I only had a glimpse, but it was enough to confirm that it was the same buck. On the other two trips through that cover, we didn't see the buck, but I did notice his fresh, large bed and that he was really starting to rub when we hunted it in mid-October.

It was the fifth day of the firearms deer season and things had not gone quite as I had planned. I had seen two good bucks but failed to get a shot at the first one and just plain missed the other. A good buck gets to be harder to come by as the season progresses, and I was mentally going over my

Rolling the dice and crowding close to a buck's bedding area could mean you bump him. It could also result in you seeing a sight like this when he gets up for a stretch.

95

not look in my direction—not until I ever-so-slowly attempted to raise the shotgun. He snapped his head in my direction, and I threw the familiar stock to my shoulder, slapping the trigger in the same instant that the buck left the ground. He made three bounds and died. When I walked over to him, I took a good look. Eight points, long tines, good mass, 17 inches inside. It was the same buck all right. You were wrong, old man, I whispered, as I reached for my knife.

DEATH OF A MYTH

A whitetail buck spends 70 percent of his life bedded. Yet we hunters spend nearly all of our time hunting everything except bedding areas. The biggest reason we avoid bedding areas is the proliferation of misinformation. The old man I met in the woods that day so many years ago and every hunter and outdoor writer since who has spouted off verbally or in print about how a buck will abandon his bedding area if disturbed has been dead wrong. It's time to put an end to this long-standing, buck-saving myth.

———⟋∘⟋∘⟋﹦———

"A deer that has been disturbed in its bedding area does not forever abandon that area."

———⟋∘⟋∘⟋﹦———

Most whitetails today live in close proximity to human beings. Some have become backyard pests. If a deer were to abandon a favored bedding site each time it was disturbed by a squirrel hunter, grouse hunter, turkey hunter, deer hunter, berry picker, mushroom hunter, bird watcher, logger, farmer, hiker or kid on a mountain bike, it would soon end up a nomadic insomniac! Even in wilderness areas, where deer have far less contact with human beings, a deer that has been disturbed in its bedding area does not forever abandon that area. In fact, it has been my experience that, if anything, wilderness deer are less concerned with these disturbances than deer that inhabit more populated regions.

When it comes to bedding habits, a mature whitetail buck or doe is much like you and me. We can sleep in a motel bed, a cabin or on a cot in a tent when we are traveling, but we sleep best in our own beds; we are most comfortable there. Mature deer tend to bed in the same places day after day, week after week, month after month, year after year. Usually they will have two or three bedding areas in their loosely defined home areas. The bed they choose on any given day is determined by the wind. Mature deer almost always bed with the wind at their backs. This allows them to

Generally, hunting near a bedding area is an all-day affair. You might be able to lure a buck to you, but patience is your most important tool.

options when I remembered the buck Old Jack and I had jumped in the aspens while grouse hunting. The wind was steady out of the north, perfect for still-hunting the aspen ridge, and three inches of new snow overnight ensured quiet footing. Dressed in wool, I slipped quietly into the south end of the aspens just before noon. Two hours later, I was nearing the north end of the ridge. Although I had seen a number of fresh beds and lots of tracks, none of the sign looked big enough to belong to the buck I had seen. The old man was probably right, I thought to myself. This old buck probably got tired of Jack and me tramping through here hunting grouse and moved out. And then the buck stood up from behind a deadfall.

He had sensed my presence. I don't know how. The wind was in my favor and the snow quiet as cotton underfoot. He had not seen me, I am sure, because when he stood he did smell any danger sneaking in from behind. They use their eyes and ears to watch and listen for intruders downwind.

The country near my home in southeast Minnesota where I spend many days each fall hunting deer is rugged hill country. Here, mature deer tend to bed just over the downwind crest of a ridge. Again, the wind carries the scent of any hunter slipping up the opposite slope, and the deer can easily spot any hunter approaching from below. Bucks especially are fond of bedding on little knobs and projections jutting off the main ridge. In flat country were deer cannot use elevation to their advantage, a mature buck will usually bed in some nasty tangle of briar and bramble better suited to a cottontail rabbit. Of all the whitetail's daily habits, his bedding behavior is the easiest to pattern and yet the one facet of his life we hunters key on the least.

A person who spent 70 percent of his or her life in bed would be called lazy, but in the whitetail's case, spending nearly three-fourths of its life bedded has nothing to do with laziness and everything to do with survival. In fact, every aspect of the whitetail's behavior is geared toward survival. That is what makes a mature whitetail the number one trophy in North America. A deer is most vulnerable when it is up and moving about. Each time a deer travels from bedding area to food source and back again, checks on its scrapes or attempts to sneak away from other hunters, it is vulnerable. Tucked away securely in its bed, it is rarely threatened. This is why nature has seen to it that the whitetail is a ruminant

"Mature deer almost always bed with the wind at their backs."

with a four-compartment stomach. If food is reasonably plentiful, a whitetail will fill the first of those four compartments in a half hour and then retire to its bed to regurgitate and chew its cud. The less time a deer spends feeding and the more time it can spend bedded, the better the deer's chances of survival.

Gun hunters can especially benefit by intruding into a buck's bedroom. Get the wind, move slowly and keep your eyes peeled.

The author with a blackpowder buck caught napping.

HOW DEER SLEEP

Deer do not sleep like you and me. Rarely will a deer enter a deep sleep; if it does it will last only minutes. Deer are like my mother-in-law watching TV in the evening—they tend to doze a lot. I've watched them many times contentedly chewing their cuds, their eyes about half closed. Most of the time their heads are upright, but in very cold weather, a deer will curl up like a dog to conserve heat while bedded. When a deer is very tired, like a buck that has been chasing does all night, he will often lie with its head tucked on his shoulder.

As an infantryman in Vietnam, I vividly recall being awakened on many nights by someone just lightly touching my shoulder, the signal that the VC or NVA were very close and that all hell was about to break loose. It is amazing how

you can go from sleep to combat-ready in one frantic heartbeat under such circumstances. The same is true of deer when they are bedded. They might look all dreamy-eyed and nonchalant, but those looks are deceiving. A whitetail's senses never sleep. In fact, a bedded deer is the most difficult deer to approach undetected.

Only three times, in a lifetime spent in their pursuit, have I successfully stalked and killed a bedded whitetail. Twice it was with a muzzleloader, which made the stalk easier since I could take the shot from 100 yards. Yet I spent $2^1/2$ hours crawling on my belly in below-zero temperatures to complete one of those stalks. But the one that is most satisfying was the buck bedded beneath a cedar tree on a ridge not far from my home. I spotted him from my vehicle as I drove to my stand that afternoon. It was very cold, something like minus 20, as I recall. I knew that my odds of pulling off the stalk were somewhere between slim and none, but somehow stalking seemed more appealing than spending a couple of hours freezing my butt off on stand. It took just over two hours, but I made it. I was 16 steps from the buck when I released the arrow.

Stalking bucks in their beds or still-hunting them in their bedding areas is great fun, but most of the time the deer will win. Drives and stand hunting are far more productive tactics for hunting bucks in their bedrooms.

BEDROOM DRIVES

Many hunters are reluctant to push a buck's bedroom because they are convinced it is a one-shot deal. Either you get the buck on that drive or you never see him again. But that is not the case. I've proven it to myself several times.

The most vivid example of this I can share with you takes place on the Republican River in southwest Nebraska. My friend, Marvin Briegel, owns a farm there, and the Republican runs right through his corn and soybean fields. There is some timber and slough ground along the river and along the little ditches and creeks that feed the river. The deer bed in these strips of cover. The fact that the deer bed in long, narrow corridors of cover instead of large blocks of timber makes Marvin's farm my favorite place in the whole world for two- and three-person deer drives.

One year, a couple of buddies and I spent seven days hunting Marvin's farm during the December muzzleloader season. We have divided the farm up into five small, manageable drives. Each day we make two and never more than three drives. Marvin knows where the deer bed and where they go when they're disturbed. Invariably we see the same deer or at least the same bucks on each drive. You get to know them after awhile: the nine-pointer with the crooked left brow tine, the spindly eight with the broken G-2, the 10 with the bleached white rack that will be a real bruiser next season. We push them out, they wander around a bit and then circle right back in again, just like a flock of mallards jumped out of a flooded cornfield.

THE BEDROOM WATCH

Once I make the decision to hunt a buck in his bedroom, I take every precaution to ensure that the buck does not suspect an intruder lurking in his place of sanctuary. When possible, I hang a stand in the bedding area months before the season, but since I travel to hunt most of the season, this is not always feasible. More often, I will discover a buck's bedding area, either intentionally or accidentally during the season. Sometimes I actually jump the buck and get a look at him, other times I rely on big beds, big tracks, big droppings and big rubs. All of that "big" sign tells me that this is a place worth hunting. When I find such a place, I hang a stand and vacate the area.

When the wind is right I hike to my stand well before dawn and get comfortable. I bring extra clothing, lots of food, something to drink and a pee bottle. Some hunters like to bring a paperback book to read. When I hunt a bedding area from a stand, I am there for the day. I will sit all day and not get down from my stand until I'm sure the buck has made his move to evening feed. Hunting a bedding area takes a heaping helping of patience. If the buck does not show during the pink light of pre-dawn—the best time—it is easy to convince yourself that it is not worth sitting the rest of the day. And it might not be. But if you

climb down and walk from the bedding area and if the buck is present and hears or sees you vacate your stand, after you are gone he will come and investigate. He is not stupid. He might not vacate his bedding area, but he will avoid your stand site. You won't know it, but you will be wasting your time hunting that stand from then on. That is why sitting all day is so important.

"We push them out, they wander around a bit and then circle right back in again ..."

And though the early-morning hours offer the best chance, don't give up if you don't see him then; the buck will not stay bedded all day. On the average, a buck will get up every couple of hours. Sometimes he will just stretch cramped muscles and relieve himself before lying back down, but other times he will wander around a bit, maybe grabbing a bite to eat or sparring with a sapling. Your chance might come at noon. Or it might happen late afternoon when the buck will stir and prepare for the evening feeding period. Sit tight and believe that it will happen.

Don't be afraid to hunt a buck in his bedroom. It is not sacred ground. Many times, invading the privacy of a buck's bedroom is the only way you stand a chance of laying eyes on him.

Do Not Disturb

There is a period of time each fall when it is a waste of time to hunt a buck's bedroom. During the actual breeding phase of the rut, mature bucks are almost constantly in the company of an estrous doe. During this time the buck goes where the doe goes, beds when and where the doe beds. Intent only upon procreation of the species, the buck forgets all about his own bedding area until his mission has been accomplished for another year.

During the weeks leading up to the actual breeding phase of the rut, the buck will spend an increasing number of the daylight hours on the move, making scrapes and rubs, checking scrapes, wandering from one group of does to the next in his search for a hot doe. A buck's bedroom is not a "bad" place to hunt during this period because the buck will periodically visit his bedding site, but there are better places to intercept a buck during this exciting part of the season.

To Call or Not to Call

by Bill Winke

Whitetail calling has received a lot of publicity. With such coverage, one would think the tactic is a sure-fire trophy producer. That would be incorrect. Calling is just one more hunting technique that can, and does, produce action when it's used at the right time and in the right place.

Calling is a part of the overall big buck game plan, not the entire game plan in itself. Maybe I'm a little backward, and maybe I'm missing out on a few opportunities, but I really don't call a whole lot. Most of the time I don't even carry rattling horns.

There are two schools of thought in calling deer. I subscribe to the low-impact school. I don't want to draw attention to myself, because I believe most big bucks that respond to calling will circle downwind and catch your scent or movement before you even know they are around. Such an education just makes an already-wary animal that much harder to hunt, especially in the immediate area.

This doesn't mean I won't call. I just don't do much blind calling. I don't hesitate to call to a big buck that I can see, especially if he's already on the verge of passing out of range. If you see a shooter during the rut, you better do everything you can to get him right now because your chances of seeing him again are relatively poor. I use the grunt call under these conditions and grunt as loudly as it takes to get his attention. Usually the buck will freeze and look my way. One or two more grunts will get him started in my direction if he's going to come at all. If he stops, I'll call again. Sometimes it works, more often it doesn't, but you've got nothing to lose in trying.

"I don't hesitate to call to a big buck that I can see, especially if he's already on the verge of passing out of range."

LEARNING BODY LANGUAGE

Under the best of conditions, where a lone buck is moseying this way and that, your chances of bringing him in are pretty good. I'd say that approximately one out of every three or four big bucks I call to under these conditions will turn and at least start toward me. About half of them actually make it all the way into bow range. That's a high success rate. I think it has to do with the buck's frame of mind at the time. When they are alone during the rut and not heading for any place in particular, they seem to respond well to calling. I'm not sure what emotion the grunt call stirs in their souls, but that it works can't be denied.

My success rate on bucks on the move, seemingly headed toward someplace in particular, is much lower—probably something like one in eight or 10. They don't seem to want to take the time or expend the effort to detour and check me out. To tell you the truth, that's when a little rattling might come in handy. (This is probably where I'm missing a few opportunities by not carrying horns and trying to charge up those bucks with more aggressive calling.)

My technique is what I would label as "last resort" calling. Under some conditions it is by far the best method to use. For example, some hunters in heavily hunted eastern states

A grunt tube is effective for stopping a moving buck in an opening, where you can make a clean shot.

only have a few acres to hunt each fall. Under those conditions, it wouldn't be smart to educate all the deer around by constantly calling. It would be better to become a part of the woods carefully and quietly and await your opportunity.

On the other hand, when you have lots of ground to hunt, you can afford to be more aggressive. Look at the hunters who specialize in rattling up big bucks down in Texas. On a big ranch you can rattle and move and rattle and move—all day long—until you contact the one big boy that's in the right frame of mind to come on in. So what if you educate a few bucks along the way? There's plenty of room and

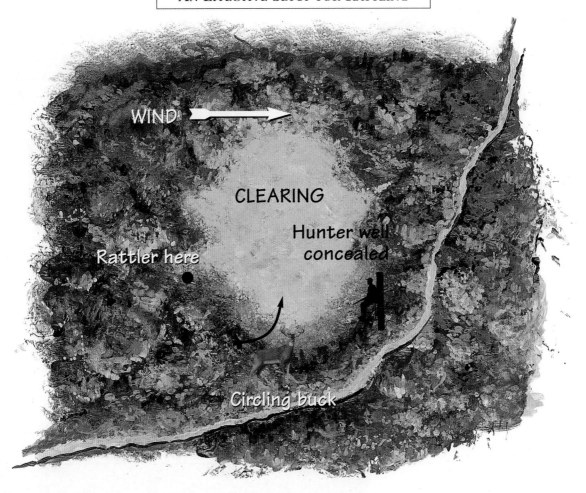

WIND

CLEARING

Hunter well concealed

Rattler here

Circling buck

When rattling, hunt in tandem to take advantage of a buck's tendency to circle downwind. The rattler sets up directly upwind of a small clearing while the hunter conceals himself directly downwind and waits for a close-range shot. The goal is to get the buck to circle downwind of the rattling and into the open where he may present a shot to the concealed hunter.

Keep your bow at the ready when you touch the horns together. If you catch the right buck in the right mood, he might come in fast.

lots more bucks where they came from. Under these conditions, blind calling, and lots of it, is a good strategy.

DIALING LONG DISTANCE

Gary Roberson, owner of Texas-based Burnham Brothers Game Calls, has been rattling up bucks in the Lone Star State for nearly three decades.

"On ranches with buck-to-doe ratios of one buck to four does (or narrower), rattling will produce good results," Roberson says. "The bucks must be competitive. I remember rattling up one buck that came in at a run. He was a real fighter. Every point on his rack was broken off! Each deer has a personality. Only the more aggressive bucks will respond to rattling in this way; others will slip in on the downwind side and still others won't respond at all.

"I like to start rattling as early as the middle of October, but the best action is in the end of November down here. I'll change my calling style to match the conditions. Early in the season I'll do more ticking of the tines to simulate sparring. Later I'll rattle very aggressively. People who hunt with me are amazed at how hard I go at it, but I've found that the more aggressive I am, the more aggressive the buck will be. I recommend rattling in pairs with a hunter and a caller. Always continue rattling until the buck is in range because if you stop, he'll stop. Stay hidden by trying to rattle behind a bush or some other type of cover and try to keep your hands and the horns hidden. I once had a buck jump right into a bush with me! I had to protect myself!"

In a typical day, Gary will walk and rattle over a large area. In good spots he'll wait half an hour, otherwise he only spends about 15 minutes. On his very best day he rattled up 12 bucks before noon! To Roberson, the setup is critical.

"When I'm rattling for a bowhunter, I'll set the hunter across a small opening downwind from me," he says. "Bucks will try to circle the clearing to catch my scent and run into the hunter. When a buck looks up, I'll grunt to him. If he looks up again, I'll stick one antler above the brush so he can see it. Murray Burnham taught me that trick many years ago." (See diagram on page 102.)

RATTLING FOR STAND HUNTERS

While moving and rattling is surely the ultimate way to present your calling to the maximum number of bucks, few of us outside of Texas or the Canadian prairies (and to a lesser extent, the Great Plains states) have access to enough ground to make that work. Most of us are calling from tree-stands and rarely get down and move to a new spot after each sequence. Stan Potts, of central Illinois, has rattled up some monsters. In fact, Potts's personal best, a huge 11-pointer that netted $195\frac{5}{8}$ Pope and Young Club points as a typical, was rattled back in 1983, at a time when few hunters outside of Texas were doing much rattling. His giant buck could well be the biggest buck ever rattled in by a bowhunter.

"It was the day after the first gun season had ended," Potts describes, "November 21st, to be exact. I got to my stand at about 2:30 in the afternoon, and at 3 p.m. I rattled for about 30 seconds and then hung my antlers up. I heard a sound and looked to see a squirrel. I turned away and heard another sound from the same direction. I just figured it was the squirrel again. When I looked back you can imagine my shock when the biggest buck that I've ever seen was standing there only 50 yards away. He was all dark and blown up, with his hair standing straight up. The giant buck dropped his head and started walking toward a thicket.

"I knew there were only two trails through the thicket, and when he came into the open again he would be either 20 yards away or 40 yards away. I turned into position and got ready. He was on the 20-yard trail. He went behind a red haw tree, and I drew my bow. He stopped behind the tree, and all I could see was the buck's nose. A few seconds later he was walking again. When he stepped out he was quartering away and was also sharply downhill from me, so I aimed high and back to hit his vitals. On the release, the arrow sunk to the fletching, right where I was aiming. That's when I started really getting nervous. I began second-guessing myself. 'Did I shoot too far back?' But I knew it was a good hit. After only about five or 10 minutes I climbed down and went back to town for help.

"Always continue rattling until the buck is in range because if you stop, he'll stop."

"We had good blood for about 50 yards, but with the high entry angle and no exit hole, almost all the bleeding was internal. We lost the blood in a grass field. I started to circle back toward where the buck had come from, shining the flashlight out in front of me. That's when I saw a huge antler sticking up above the grass. He had only gone about 125 yards and had died seconds after the arrow hit him."

Today Potts still does a lot of rattling during the rut. "I wouldn't think of going hunting without my horns," he says.

Stan Potts with a rattled-up buck. Not bad, huh?

Three rattling tools: Real antlers, rattling box, rattling bag.

"I start rattling about the last week of October. I think the pre-rut and right after the peak are the best times to rattle.

"I don't do anything special. I don't think it's possible to actually imitate the sounds of two bucks fighting, but you really don't have to. They come to it anyway. I smack the horns together hard when I start a sequence, just to get the attention of any bucks within hearing range. I rattle for about 1½ minutes and then quickly hang the horns up and grab my bow. I wait 15 minutes and then rattle for another 30 seconds or so. I might wait another hour before starting another sequence. I rattle all day long while I'm on stand. I also keep a grunt call handy to call to bucks that hang up out of range after coming to the rattling."

Potts admitted that his success rate is not overly high. "I call in a buck maybe one out of every 15 to 20 times that I rattle," he says. "Most of those are subordinates. But every once in awhile I'll bring in a real dandy. I also like to rattle to deer that I see passing out of range because I feel that rattling can be heard farther away than grunt calls."

Calling and rattling are personal decisions. You sure don't have to call or rattle to take trophy bucks. On the other hand, if the conditions permit, there is no reason not to. If only one wallhanger is tagged in your hunting lifetime directly as a result of rattling or grunting, it is well worth the effort.

WHEN THE RUT IS GONE

by David Morris

I've tried hard to find a way around it, but I regretfully must admit that the post-rut period is the most difficult time to hunt trophy whitetails, especially if they're subjected to much hunting pressure. They are now perfectly content to while away their daylight hours in the security of thick cover if bothered by people. In fact, even if not disturbed, older bucks are going to be largely nocturnal during this time. The post-rut is a somewhat complex time period and can be divided into three different stages based on behavioral patterns.

The first is what I call the *waning rut*. This stage includes both the tail-off breeding activity immediately following the peak breeding period and the relatively minor secondary rut. The greatest activity of the waning rut occurs during the first three to four weeks of the post-rut period. These last flurries of breeding activity probably represent the best chance a hunter has for a trophy during the post-rut period.

The second stage is what I call the *post-rut lull,* and for good reason: Bucks are lying low in thick cover and recuperating from the rigors of the rut. They can seem to virtually disappear from the face of the earth during this stage.

The third and last stage occurs when the bucks return to a feeding pattern. Prospects brighten somewhat now, depending on hunting pressure, the availability of prime food sources, herd density and the severity of the winter. But before looking at these three stages, let's explore the timing and length of the post-rut period.

TIMING AND DURATION

The post-rut period starts when the two-week breeding period ends. Therefore, the timing of the post-rut can be determined by adding two weeks to the starting date of the breeding period. The beginning of the post-rut period is marked by a dramatic decline in breeding activity, though remnant breeding seems to continue for awhile.

The close of the post-rut is brought about by a specific event: antler shedding. When bucks drop their antlers can vary greatly from region to region and can even vary somewhat from year to year within the same area. Obviously, when peak rut occurs is the key factor affecting regional timing, but the condition of the bucks contributes to year-to-year variances at a given locale. Generally, the better the bucks' condition, or put another way, the less stressed, the later they drop their antlers.

———⟨∘⁄∘⟩———

"The post-rut period starts when the two-week breeding period ends."

———⟨∘⁄∘⟩———

The most prevalent time throughout the country for antler-shedding is January through mid-February. Montana whitetails, for instance, have pretty much lost their antlers by mid-January. However, South Texas bucks drop their antlers much later—in March and even early April. Bucks in Alabama, where the rut is very late, don't normally lose their antlers until March. Frankly, when the post-rut ends and exactly how long it lasts are of little concern to hunters since few places have hunting seasons extending to the end of the post-rut period.

THE WANING RUT

As the peak rut comes to an end, breeding and its related activities begin to wind down. With fewer does in heat, the general chaos eases. During the first couple of weeks of the waning rut, breeding activity is dependent upon the late arrivals to estrus, the number of which diminishes steadily as time passes. Still, the bucks are hopeful and remain focused primarily on breeding. When the bucks start having trouble picking up hot does, they range out looking for receptive does, anxiously checking the doe groups. Their travel pattern is somewhat like that of the scraping period, only less predictable, more nocturnal and accompanied by much less sign making. They are now looking directly for a willing doe and depend on their noses to reveal her presence.

About two weeks into the post-rut period, the dwindling breeding activity can get a shot in the arm by the arrival of the secondary rut. If this second cycle, made up mostly of 1½-year-old does, is significant, the breeding ritual is again played out on a mini-scale. Overall activity is, however, far less widespread. Much of the limited breeding activity takes place at night, the cumulative results of growing weariness and ongoing hunting pressure. From the hunter's perspective, visible rutting activity will be isolated and sporadic, and fresh buck sign will be sparse.

About a month into the period, the waning rut is pretty much over. With each passing day that a buck doesn't score, his enthusiasm wanes. Gradually, rutting activity gives way to resting or brief periods of feeding. The buck's travels become less extensive. Doe groups drop off his route. The buck soon drifts back to his core area and starts passing the daylight hours bedded in his familiar territory. Slowly, the urge to breed loses its grip on him, and the need to rest and recover from the rigors of the rut takes priority. Only the alluring scent of a hot doe can rekindle the fire in a rut-weary buck. Maybe it's an isolated late doe that comes into estrus and rearranges

Sometimes a doe isn't bred during the normal rut days and will cycle into heat again. When this happens, it can cause a brief flurry of buck activity.

One adult buck can breed many does during the rut. When the rut winds down, he'll likely be in poor physical condition and will spend a week or more recuperating and traveling very little.

his schedule. Or perhaps it's the minor third cycle, which usually hits about six weeks into the post-rut period and consists mostly of six-month-old doe fawns, that brings that familiar, all-powerful scent back to the deer woods. Even then, the effects are limited and short-lived.

THE POST-RUT LULL

As the power of the rut relaxes its hold, the post-rut lull sets in. Deer begin the shift to a quieter, more settled lifestyle. Cold, rain and/or snow have reduced the amount of secure cover available to deer. The leaves have fallen off the trees, the underbrush has been denuded, and the tall grass is laid low. The food supply, once fairly well distributed over much of the deer's range, is now diminished both in quantity and distribution. The deer, haggard and skittish, feel the stress and fatigue brought on by the frantic pace of the previous weeks. Their priority now becomes rest and food. They seek refuge in the remaining pockets of thick, secure cover and devote more time and attention to nourishing their neglected bodies.

Does, fawns and young bucks come through the rut in

fairly good shape physically and quickly return to something resembling a regular feeding pattern, perhaps bedding in thick pockets of cover near the food source during the day and feeding at first and last light and at night. Hunting pressure will determine the level of daytime activity.

With mature bucks, the routine immediately following the last days of significant breeding is different. Having neglected both food and rest, they now find themselves exhausted. For a time, their drive to feed takes a back seat to their desire for rest and solitude. The older bucks, already back in their core area, seek out the thickest or most secure areas to bed. Their privacy and rest assured, they will feed some, but mostly at night and near their beds. As far as the hunter is concerned, mature bucks often seem to cease to exist in the midst of the post-rut lull.

It's hard to say how long the lull lasts. Remnant breeding activity tends to override and confuse the pattern, as does hunting pressure. Movement and sign are so limited that figuring out exactly what deer are doing is difficult. The severity of the climate (the cold), the physical condition of the deer and, of course, hunting pressure are all factors in how long it takes adult bucks to return to a consistent feeding pattern. My guess is that this recuperation time usually lasts from one to two weeks before giving way to a consistent feeding pattern.

---◁◦◦◦▷---

"Mature bucks often seem to cease to exist in the midst of the post-rut lull."

---◁◦◦◦▷---

THE FEED BAG

In time, rut-weary bucks slowly regain their strength by resting long hours and feeding on food sources convenient to their bedding areas. Winter is upon them, and the bucks feel the need to nourish themselves in preparation for the hard times ahead. Gradually, their daily routine shifts. They venture out farther and farther from their core areas in search of quality food. If preferred agricultural crops are in the area, you can be sure that most bucks eventually will end up feeding there. Clearcuts and other concentrated food sources will also draw their attention. In the absence of con-

centrated feed, the deer scatter over the entire range and forage as best they can. The feeding pattern now is much like that of the pre-rut period except that the bucks are more nocturnal, food sources are fewer and more localized and the deer might have to travel even farther for prime feed. The hunting prospects during this time depend largely on the presence of major food sources to concentrate deer and on hunting pressure.

Concentrations of deer can be phenomenal during the late post-rut, especially in the cold latitudes and among overcrowded populations. (Fortunately for the deer, hunting season is seldom in when these concentrations occur.) I've seen situations where deer from miles around seem to converge on a major food source. Their quest for food might even cause them to abandon their core areas for a time and relocate miles away near prime food sources. An extreme example of this is the actual whitetail migrations that take place in the mountainous regions of the West. Severe winter weather and deep snows also can cause deer in harsh northern climates to concentrate in the limited protective cover. This is called "yarding." We won't focus on yarding per se since deer are seldom hunted at such times. I mention it because this extreme behavior is somewhat indicative of what deer across the country do in the late post-rut period. They will bunch up in the best available cover, although to a far less exaggerated degree than in classic yarding.

Bucks will stay near the does for a few days after the rut winds down, but then they will split for a place of security with nearby food.

In middle Georgia, for instance, deer "herd up" in pockets of thick evergreens in impressive numbers after winter has "burned" the cover back. They spend most of their time in these protective pockets of cover, venturing out only to feed. I've seen this same situation everywhere I've hunted, except in places such as South Texas, Florida and the coastal "jungles" of the South where widespread cover is maintained even during the winter. This tendency toward yarding during the post-rut period creates an ideal situation for driving deer. The only problem is that trophy bucks aren't always bedded with the large concentrations of deer found in the obvious pockets of cover.

HUNTING THE POST-RUT

Hunting the post-rut is not an enviable task, especially when trophy bucks are the goal. Where pressure is high, the deer probably have been shot at, run off their feeding grounds, kept awake during their daily nap times and even disturbed on "hot dates." Under such conditions, even does, fawns and young bucks will resort almost totally to nocturnal sorties, and you certainly won't find mature bucks up and about of their own accord in the daylight. The more pressure, the more reclusive and nocturnal the deer become and the longer it takes them to return to normal activity.

During the first three to four weeks of the post-rut, the best game in town is the low-level rutting activity brought on by latecomers from the first breeding cycle and by the secondary rut. The strategy is about the same as for the breeding period—hunt the doe concentrations, preferably those where big buck sign can be found, even if it's not too fresh. Unfortunately, bucks don't leave much sign during the post-rut. The best evidence of rutting activity is to actually see a buck trailing or chasing. If you see this, hunt the area hard. There could be several bucks, including the local "big cheese," working the vicinity in hopes of connecting with one of the relatively few does now in heat.

"The more pressure, the more reclusive and nocturnal the deer become and the longer it takes them to return to normal activity."

If I believe a hot doe is in the area, I prefer to slip quietly through the woods in search of the breeding party. Stand hunting is better if no rutting activity is evident since deer are very skittish now. Rattling can work during the waning rut, but results will be spotty. In fact, I've actually seen bucks

Your days are numbered after the breeding is complete. Post-rut buck sign is often difficult to find and more difficult to hunt effectively.

run from rattling during the post-rut. On the other hand, I've had some success by rattling rather modestly in one spot and then waiting patiently for long periods, which for me is 20 to 30 minutes. Unless a hot doe is around to fire the bucks up, I've found that post-rut bucks respond very cautiously and usually prefer to scent check some distance downwind rather than approach the fake fight directly as they might earlier.

If forced movement is ever the best way to hunt trophy whitetails, it is during the post-rut lull. I employ two different hunting tactics to force movement during this time. One, I slip ever so slowly through thickets that are likely big buck bedding areas. Three good things can come from this. I might jump a buck and get a quick shot. A buck might stand up and hold momentarily for a shot upon hearing a slight noise or seeing an unidentifiable movement. Or I might catch an unsuspecting buck loitering around in his bedding area. Of course, a number of bad things can happen, and they considerably outweigh the good. That aside, I have killed a couple of trophy bucks using this rather desperate tactic. However, I confess that my return on investment is

Dressing for the Cold

How many times have you been sitting on a deer stand wishing for a warmer pair of boots, gloves or—better yet—a heater!

Late-season deer hunting is demanding both mentally and physically. Deer sightings are generally down compared to during the regular firearms or bow season, and the weather in many locations across the whitetail's range can get downright brutal. Ever been in a Michigan or Minnesota stand in December? How about Saskatchewan at minus 20ºF? Who says this deer hunting stuff is fun? Well, it still can be if you are outfitted for the late-season elements.

In many cases, the key to staying warm is staying dry. That means warding off snow and wicking away sweat. Many deer hunters fall victim to cold because they put on every stitch of clothing before they ever step out of the truck. It's a nice feeling for the first few steps, but by the time you've covered the couple hundred yards to your stand, you're sweating profusely. An hour later you can't stand the cold and are forced to head for the truck. A guideline to remember is that you should dress for the walk so that you'll feel "cool" starting out. Carry the rest of your outerwear in a pack and dress after you arrive at your stand and cool down. That way, you'll avoid breaking out in a sweat.

Cotton long underwear is a sure way to get cold fast. Long underwear made of Thermax or polypropylene will help to wick moisture away from your skin. Look for the same characteristics in the socks you choose for cold-weather hunts.

If you're not dressed properly, you won't be out there hunting. And if you're not hunting, you won't be shooting any deer.

Intermediate layers of PolarTec and Thinsulate and clothing that uses W.L. Gore's Windstopper membrane will help to hold body heat while letting moisture escape. And these types of garments perform at a high level with less bulk. For bowhunters especially, this is an important consideration. Consider vests to keep your chest warm while allowing good freedom of movement.

Outer garments are a matter of choice. Many veteran deer hunters still swear by wool and with good reason: wool sheds moisture and has excellent insulating qualities. If you choose something other than wool, try to select a garment that is waterproof and quiet in addition to providing good insulation. From there, good headgear like a balaclava will hold heat in around your head and neck. A handwarmer muff strapped around your waist and plenty of disposable heat packs will keep hands warm during all-day sits. A quality pac boot should be sized one size too large to allow your foot to move within the boot even while wearing a wicking sock and wool sock. And to protect your feet even further, consider the insulated blanket overboots on the market.

Finally, some hunters even tote a sleeping bag along to the deer stand and pull it up to their chest once they've settled in. It's not a warm sofa in front of the fireplace, but you can't kill a big buck at home.

—Gregg Gutschow

meager when invading a buck's bedding area.

MICRO-HUNTING

The other tactic to force movement is deer drives. There is no other time of year when deer drives are as justified. There are times and situations during the post-rut period when deer simply won't move unless you move them. The success of deer drives now depends on knowing where big bucks might be bedded.

The post-rut lull is the time for what I call "micro-hunting." Let me explain. During the scraping and breeding periods particularly, bucks are on the move and can cover lots of country, sometimes even exposing themselves in the relative open during full daylight. It is generally to the hunter's advantage during such times to look over as much deer habitat as possible. Not so after the tail-off breeding has wound down and the lull has set in. During this time, mature bucks don't move much or travel far in the daytime, and what movement there is normally takes place in thick cover. This forces the hunter to focus on thick-cover sanctuaries and pinpoint a specific spot to ambush a buck within the relatively small area that he's likely to be moving about in. This is micro-hunting and, to be honest, it's not my cup of tea. You can see why I said earlier that the best bet is to take advantage of the remnant breeding activity early in the period.

Hunting in close quarters leaves no room for mistakes. A favorable wind and total quiet are essential. I'll often take a seat next to a sizable tree rather than risk making noise while hanging a stand. Hunting like this is slow and tedious. But if

When breeding tails off and bad weather rolls in, bucks move less and stick to the thick cover. Take these factors into account.

you want to shoot a big buck now, hunting them where they are—in the thickets—is not a bad idea. As always, don't pick a stand site randomly. Find some sort of sign that says a good buck is frequenting the area.

LAST WORDS

When mature bucks settle into a feeding pattern during the post-rut period, a hunter's options increase, assuming deer season is still open, which is seldom the case. The hunting strategy called for is essentially the same employed during the pre-rut period. In pressured areas, emphasis should be placed on hunting the staging grounds near major food sources or trails leading to and from bedding/feeding areas. As a general rule, the higher the pressure, the closer to the bedding area and the denser the cover you'll need to hunt. Conversely, the lower the pressure, the closer to the food source you should hunt. In very low-pressure situations, even hunting open food sources might be productive.

Considerable scouting might be needed during the post-rut period to find the best place to wait out a buck headed to food. Stand hunting is the most reliable way to hunt bucks on a feeding pattern. Still-hunting can also be effective if conditions are right, but deer are easily spooked now and difficult to sneak up on. Hunt to the last legal minute of the day and be in position in the morning before first light. Try to find bottlenecks or some physical feature to help funnel a buck your way. Even if you do everything right, you'll still need a large dose of patience and a double dose of luck to kill a big buck during the post-rut!

Chapter 4

IN SEARCH
OF OLD BUCKS

Trophy hunters raise the bar to dizzying heights with their unwavering discipline and painstaking hunting. Pursuit of trophy whitetails must be a personal choice, a trail chosen only when we are truly ready. For this treacherous journey takes us to whitetail hunting extremes.

Hundreds of deer, some of them fine bucks, will walk on. We are waiting, planning, pursuing. Hunting trophy whitetails is a test of will. And those who enter the whitetail woods after a particular deer often come home with an empty tag and a heightened respect for old bucks.

It can become obsession. Winter scouting. Shed hunting in spring. Scanning summer fields for bucks wearing thick, velvet-covered antlers.

What are trophy hunters really chasing? A dream. A dream that one day everything happens as imagined. A giant whitetail buck steps into view. And you find yourself frozen in one of big game hunting's finest moments.

Here's to dreams of giant whitetails ...

ARE THEY DIFFERENT?

by David Morris

Trophy bucks are different and very special. They are so different, in fact, from lesser bucks and does that they might as well be an entirely separate species. And unless hunters recognize that and hunt accordingly, they simply will not take trophy bucks with any consistency. With that in mind, two questions arise. One, what is a trophy whitetail? Two, how are they different? Let's try to answer those questions.

The term "trophy whitetail" can be defined on two different levels. The first is the personal level, which is based on pride of accomplishment and might have absolutely nothing to do with size. No one can dispute it if a hunter considers a buck he shot to be a "prized memento of one's personal accomplishment," as one dictionary defines "trophy." Under this definition what constitutes a trophy varies with each hunter and is dependent on where he hunts, his hunting experience, the time available to hunt and the hunting conditions. That's why a yearling four-pointer can rightfully be considered a "trophy" by a beginner tagging his first buck.

For our purposes, however, a definition based on pride of accomplishment rather than size is much too subjective and variable. We need a more objective, size-related definition, yet one that does take into account the very real size difference in bucks from various regions across the continent. Certainly, the words "trophy buck" conjure up an image of a mature, big-racked buck in the minds of most hunters. From this collective perspective, we can define a trophy whitetail as a mature buck, at least 3½ years old, with antlers large enough to rank him among the best bucks consistently taken in a given area.

MINIMUM AGE

Why choose 3½ years as the minimum age for a mature buck? While it's true that bucks normally reach their greatest size between the ages of 5½ and 7½, only a small percentage of the bucks in North America survive to reach this age. Bucks 5½ years old and older are practically nonexistent in most deer populations, so to evaluate trophy prospects based

114

around bucks of this age would eliminate most populations from consideration. On the other hand, bucks younger than 3½ simply don't have the antler size nor the survival savvy to be called "mature" or to be given the lofty label of "trophy" by serious hunters. But a 3½-year-old can have impressive antlers and, especially when pressured, can exhibit the uncanny survival skills unique to the trophy whitetail buck.

Now, as for how trophy bucks differ and why they're so special, you need to start with the animal itself. Whitetails as a species are among the most intelligent and adaptable of all animals. What other big game animal can live, even prosper, right under the nose of man? These smart, adaptable creatures have now had a couple of hundred years of intense hunting pressure to hone to a fine edge their survival instincts, and that's the case with just your average, run-of-the-mill whitetail. Now, let's go to the smartest of the smart—trophy bucks. By nature, old, big-racked bucks are the most reclusive members of the clan, and if that weren't enough, they've been made even more reclusive by being the most sought after of their species. It's literally a matter of get smart or get dead for trophy bucks, and they've answered the call quite admirably. So admirably, in fact, that except during the rut they have very little in common with does or lesser bucks, either in their behavior or where they live. They are largely nocturnal or will become that way at the first sign of pressure. To fully understand these remarkable animals, you need to understand the aging process and the changes they go through.

You might find a young buck running with a big group of does like this, but old bucks often see danger in numbers.

—————

"A 2½-year-old in a hunted population is twice as hard to kill as that same buck at 1½ years old."

—————

HARD TARGETS

For 20 years, I managed the 13,000-acre Burnt Pine Plantation in middle Georgia. Our guests harvested close to 1,500 bucks during that time. The plantation was a great place to study and observe deer. And study them we did. Our biologists kept meticulous records of the deer sighted and harvested by guests. In addition, they conducted off-season deer censuses and, among other things, classified all bucks seen into one of three age groups—1½-, 2½- and 3½-year-old or older. Over the years, we collected vast amounts of consistent data that gave us a very accurate idea of our deer density, buck/doe ratio and, very importantly, our buck age structure. From all this, we were able to draw certain conclusions about the vulnerability of each buck age class by comparing the ages of the bucks sighted or killed by hunters with the

known buck age structure of the population. Those conclusions clearly showed the accelerating difficulty of killing a buck with each passing year.

A 1½-year-old buck is a pretty easy target. He's naive, eager and often too bold for his own good, about like a teenage boy out on his own for the first time and just discovering girls. The buck is driven by the rutting urge, but is not sure what to do about it. Yearling bucks have little compunction about moving during daylight hours and frequenting major feeding areas or any other place the crowd hangs out. Just hunt deer and you'll find 1½-year-old bucks. They differ little in vulnerability from does, except that they are more naive once you've made contact with them. Without question, the great majority of the bucks killed across the country are yearlings.

Substantial progress is made in a buck's education between 1½ and 2½, but it is only a pale foreshadowing of what is to come. The naive, almost air-headed attitude of his first year has now given way to a measured caution and the realization, just a mild suspicion, that danger might be near at any time. The 2½-year-old is strongly attracted by the lure of the rut and will demonstrate obvious confidence in the presence of does, fawns and yearlings. They tend to spend considerable time around doe groups and major food sources. They will move readily during daylight hours, but not so freely as a year earlier. Hunters after "just bucks" will bump into their share of 2½s, but bucks at this age are warier and less likely to expose themselves to a hunter's bullet than a yearling. In fact, plantation records say that a 2½-year-old in a hunted population is twice as hard to kill as that same buck at 1½ years old ... and he's only just started to wise up!

At 3½, a buck has pretty well caught on to the basics of survival but still has room to work on the fine points. With two seasons as a legal target behind and the added maturity that time and experience bring, he has learned the dangers and how to avoid them. His travels are deliberate and usually in thicker cover or under the concealment of darkness. He spends less time around the doe groups and more time in his own now-well-established core area. Still, he is vulnerable, mainly when his newfound caution is compromised by the rut, but a 3½-year-old buck is far from easy, especially in heavily hunted populations. That fact is driven home by plantation records that argue a buck is three times harder to kill at 3½ than at 2½ and six times harder to kill at 3½ than at 1½! Factor in how few bucks in most areas ever reach the ripe old age of 3½ and you realize why killing a mature buck of any size is quite an accomplishment.

If a buck makes it to 4½, the odds are slim that he'll fall to a hunter's bullet. A buck this age and older is now in the advanced program of whitetail studies. His every move and

---

"Killing a mature buck of any size is quite an accomplishment."

---

intent are governed by the drive to survive. He has few weaknesses that the hunter can exploit, and about the only time his guard is dropped, even briefly, is when the scent of a hot doe hangs heavily in the air. Outside the rut, these hunter-wise old bucks are darn near unkillable, especially if pres-

sured, in which case they will become almost totally nocturnal. If they move during daylight hours, it's a safe bet they'll be in thick cover.

Bucks that see the other side of 4½ have the hunters patterned far better than we do them. Normal tactics and long-time permanent stands don't pose much of a threat. They avoid the doe hangouts and the places frequented by other deer. They are extremely difficult to catch in the open, even on major food sources. Over the years on the plantation, bucks 4½ years old and older were so hard to come by that we couldn't even calculate meaningful odds of killing them! And it only gets worse with each passing year beyond 4½!

One on one, the trophy whitetail is unquestionably one of the most challenging animals in the world to hunt. Think about it. They live in thick cover; they are all but nocturnal; they are equipped with senses humans cannot hope to match, especially hearing and smell; they are constantly wired and ready to jump out of their skin at the slightest provocation; and, on top of all of that, their intelligence seems sufficient for them to teach school at the junior college level if only they could talk. They are just plain tough to line up in a set of sights. Anything more difficult would have to get its edge from remoteness, difficult terrain, harsh climate, scarcity, aggressiveness or a truly nocturnal nature. The fact is that without the rut to weaken their defenses, animal rights activists would probably have the trophy whitetail listed as "rare and endangered" ... and we hunters would agree with them!

Yearling bucks like these are rookies at avoiding danger. That's why they make up the bulk of the hunting harvest in many cases.

WHERE THEY LIVE

by David Morris

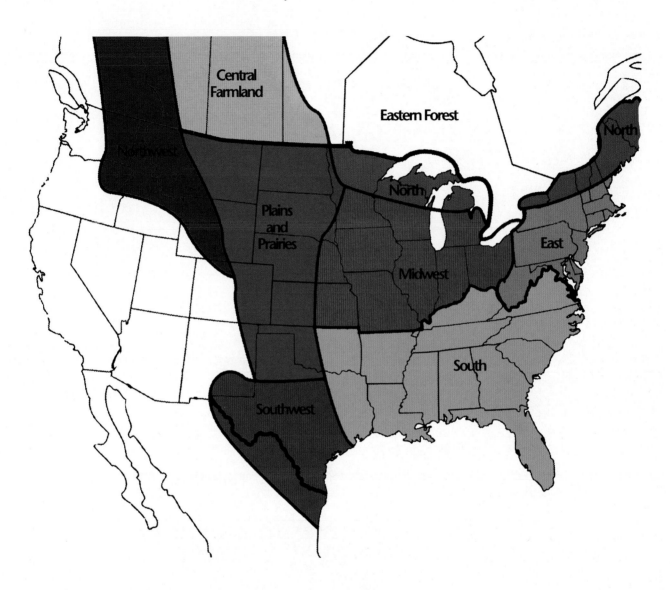

*I*n this chapter, we'll divide North America into regions based on similarity of habitat, trophy prospects, geographic location and hunting traditions. Then we'll discuss the trophy potential in each region. Obviously, our survey will be no more than a general stereotyping of what to expect within the region. The quality of trophy hunting can and does vary greatly within any given region, and we cannot possibly deal with the many exceptions.

Keep in mind that we are considering only mature bucks, i.e., those 3½ years old and older. Also, remember

that our definition of a trophy is a mature buck big enough to be among the best consistently taken in a given area.

One last note. The following information presents some trophy prospects for each region. The reason for this is that a trophy hunter is going to put forth an effort to search out a place where his chances are better than those of the masses. In all cases I looked at both worst-case scenarios and across-the-board averages. In some instances, what I saw would discourage even the most enthusiastic would-be trophy hunter. In other cases, there's cause to get real excited.

❦ NORTH: HARSH HUNTING ❦

The legendary North Country, a harsh land of cold, snow and deep evergreen forest, is steeped in deer hunting tradition. Names like the Upper Peninsula, Adirondack Mountains, Maine, Wisconsin and Minnesota all bring images of big bucks tracking through fresh snow to true whitetail aficionados. Despite its fame, hunting in the North is not easy. Lots of snow, extreme cold, rugged terrain, vast unbroken woods and low deer densities in many areas make hunting there among the hardest anywhere, but some of the biggest bucks in the country could be the payoff.

Even though pressure in this region ranges from moderate in the southern reaches to low in the northern locales, the number of mature bucks is relatively low simply because deer densities are so low. An excellent buck age structure, especially in the wilder areas, pushes the average mature buck score up to about 135. Difficult hunting conditions and low numbers make a 140 a trophy, but every year, 160-points-plus bucks are killed there. This region has the big deer; the problem is killing them. An aggressive, physically fit hunter has a definite edge when it comes to taking big bucks consistently in this challenging land.

Part of the mystique of the North Country is the expectation that something huge can walk out at any time. Indeed, a number of book deer are shot in the better areas of the region every year, and some are real whoppers.

In Minnesota and Wisconsin particularly, the trophy potential is world-class, as the record book will attest. Northern Maine, New Brunswick and Nova Scotia, all of which are poured from the same mold, have a well-deserved reputation for huge bucks. Northern New York, Vermont and New Hampshire have some good bucks but don't have the top-end size of the other areas in the region. Upper Michigan's top-end falls somewhere in the middle.

∾ EAST: UNDER PRESSURE ∾

Much of the East holds relatively little promise for the serious trophy hunter. The reason is simple—hunting pressure. Few bucks live long enough to achieve any size. Even 3½-year-old bucks are scarce in the heaviest hunted places, and anything older is rarer than an honest fisherman.

Trophy size is limited to the 100- to 130-point range and there is a low number of mature bucks, practically all of which are only 3½. A 140 would gather a crowd almost anywhere here.

Interestingly, some of the better bucks in the East are in suburban areas where hunting is restricted or off-limits. Good bucks live in the small neighborhood woodlots in Connecticut, Massachusetts, Rhode Island and even New Jersey. Since hunters don't generally have access to them (except for a few bowhunters), those deer are not considered in a discussion of trophy prospects.

Of the places available to hunters, the less pressured areas of West Virginia, Vermont and New Hampshire and some of the larger protected farms in Maryland and southern Pennsylvania offer pretty good hunting for bucks in the 120 to 135 range. But this quality is not the norm for the region. Overall, the average size of the relatively few bucks that make it to maturity is around 115, but that doesn't reflect the true size potential, even considering that they're nearly all 3½. Overcrowding has long been a problem and has drastically cut into buck size. Perhaps even more insidious is the erosion of genetic quality in certain areas due to the near total harvest of bucks with clearly visible antlers, leaving only the smallest bucks to do the breeding. Even though huntability is fairly good in the East, it doesn't help much when mature bucks are so few and far between. The serious trophy hunter there has to seek out the more remote, unhunted areas or protected private land to have consistent success.

✦ SOUTHERN CHALLENGE ✦

The hunting tradition runs deep in the South. High deer densities, long seasons, liberal bag limits and a large rural population make deer hunting an important part of Southern culture. The South is a diverse region; habitats vary from rugged mountains to vast river swamps to gently rolling hills of broken forests to flat, monoculture piney woods. Most hunting is done on private land, and trophy management of varying levels is on a rapid rise throughout the South. As a result of all this, the amount of hunting pressure differs greatly from one area to another and even from one tract to another.

Overall, pressure leans to the high side of moderate in the South. Thus, the number of mature bucks is low to moderate even though deer densities are high. In recent years the cumulative detrimental effect of overcrowding might well have surpassed even the lack of age as the greatest limiting factor in antler size. In large areas of the South the habitat has been scoured by too many deer for years, and now the nutrition necessary to produce quality antlers is simply not there. As a result of the lack of age and good nutrition, the average size of mature bucks in the South is about 110. Trophy status starts at 120, and anything over 130 is exceptional. Though bigger ones are taken there, a 140 is pretty much the realistic top-end. It was not always that way, however.

On one middle-Georgia property that I hunted, $3\frac{1}{2}$-year-old bucks commonly scored 125 to 135 and a $4\frac{1}{2}$-year-old or better was sure to crowd or top 140. On that same property today, most $3\frac{1}{2}$-year-olds score 100 to 115, and the occasional $4\frac{1}{2}$-year-old seldom breaks 130 ... all because too many mouths have been out there for too many years. That's unfortunate because the management potential to produce quality deer in the South is tremendous ... if hunters will restrain their trigger finger on young bucks and take enough does to keep the herd in check. Of course, the game departments must provide regulations that will allow enough does to be taken, which they haven't always done. On the positive side, the South has tremendous recuperative powers with its warm climate and long growing season, so it is possible to quickly remedy the ills of the past.

As for huntability, the South has to be slightly harder than average to hunt. Thick, leafy cover adds an element of difficulty to hunting. Hunting pressure, worsened in areas by dog hunting and very long seasons, causes deer to move mostly at first and last light or at night. Even the typically warm weather encourages only nocturnal movement. Without food plots or agriculture to expose and concentrate deer, the South can prove to be a fairly difficult place to hunt.

❧ EVERYTHING'S BIG IN TEXAS ❧

In the Southwest region, we'll focus on the two main areas: the Texas Hill Country and South Texas Brush Country, two of the most remarkable deer areas in the world! These two places are among the most popular destinations for traveling whitetail hunters on the continent. Both have some of the highest numbers of mature bucks found anywhere, although the size of the bucks differs greatly between the two areas. Only the riverbottoms of the Plains & Prairies region can compare with the hill country and brush country for sheer numbers of mature bucks.

The quality of hunting in general and trophy hunting in particular varies tremendously within both the hill country and brush country. The reason for this is deer management. Many ranches practice some of the most intense trophy management in the world, often including the use of game-proof fences to control the herd. Others have more modest programs that limit harvests and promote quality to varying degrees. Some places have no management at all and have depleted buck populations. Interestingly, I know of nowhere else that buck size varies so much within such close proximity as does that of the hill country and brush country.

THE HILL COUNTRY

The hill country harbors a very high number of mature bucks—even though pressure there is moderate—because the hill country has the highest concentration of whitetails in the world! It has been estimated that 10 percent of all the whitetails in North America live in the hill country! Deer densities run from 40 to an incredible 100 per square mile. Unfortunately, all these mouths to feed have taken a toll on buck size there.

While the average mature buck in the hill country scores no more than 100, their overwhelming abundance results in a good supply of bucks up to 115 or so. A 120 is a mighty fine hill country buck. A 130 is most exceptional on all but the most intensively managed ranches. The reasonable top-end is about 140. But to show what the hill country is capable of when the herd is held in check, the harvest tightly controlled and a quality food supply maintained, I have a friend who intensively manages a 1,200-acre high-fenced ranch that has produced several bucks topping 150 and a couple well into the 160s over the last half dozen years. Overall, however, I consider the hill country to be the best place on the continent to shoot a buck scoring from 90 to 120.

The hill country is highly huntable. While there are places with impenetrable stands of cedar and rugged terrain, much of the hill country consists of reasonably open live oak stands interspersed with grassy meadows. The hills themselves offer good vantage points for extended visibility. Additionally, these small Texas deer tend to move freely during daylight hours. The fact that baiting is legal and widely practiced doesn't hurt huntability, either.

The Brush Country

For the serious trophy hunter, South Texas is one of the premier trophy spots in North America. South Texas is an arid, semitropical land covered with thorny brush that doesn't look like it would support anything—but is that ever a wrong impression!

A combination of factors contributes to the extraordinary number and size of mature bucks in the South Texas brush country. One, the region consists largely of expansive ranches, many 10,000 to 25,000 acres and some more than 100,000 acres, that are closely protected and managed. Two, the soil is very fertile; thus, the scraggly-looking plants are deceptively nutritious. Three, the genetic potential for big racks is excellent, which is surprising given the extreme location. Four, although the region supports a high deer population, periodic droughts and heavy predation (especially on fawns) tend to serve as built-in mechanisms to prevent overcrowding. As a result, relatively unhunted herds can stay in balance with their habitat, which allows for the virtual stockpiling of older, bigger bucks. All these things make South Texas most unique—and the number one place in the world to shoot a buck scoring between 120 and 150!

Hunting pressure in South Texas is low, and the harvest there is the most selective anywhere. Hunters are looking for something special and seldom shoot the first buck to come along. Few immature bucks are taken if any type of management is in place. As a result, the effective hunting pressure is even lower than the actual hunter days applied. This makes for a very high population of mature bucks.

The average mature buck in the brush country pushes 130, owing to the high average age. There are plenty of 140s around. Though 150-plus bucks are starting to represent a relatively small percentage of mature bucks, the sheer number of mature bucks present results in an abundance of 150s, rivaling even the giant buck regions of the midwest and central Canada. As you move into the 160s, South Texas starts to lag behind the midwest and central Canada, but is still in the game. When it comes to book deer, South Texas doesn't stack up nearly as well either in terms of actual numbers or percentage of the buck kill. Still, South Texas does turn out several book deer a year, provided the rains hit right. For my money, the best ranches in South Texas offer the finest trophy whitetail hunting experience on earth!

Huntability varies considerably in South Texas. In the eastern coastal areas, the deer are perhaps the most naive and vulnerable anywhere. Living among live oak mottes scattered throughout open grasslands, the deer are not only highly visible but, for reasons I don't fully understand, they are exceptionally tame for a whitetail. As you move farther west into the more classic brush country, not only is the cover thicker, but the deer are wilder. By the time you get to the western edge of the brush country near the Rio Grande, the thorn brush is wall-to-wall and the bucks are spring-loaded bundles of nerves. Overall huntability in the brush country ranks somewhere in the middle of the spectrum ... except during the rut, when huntability becomes better than average because of the high competition between the many mature bucks.

MIDWEST'S BREAD-BASKET BUCKS

The Midwest, with expansive fields of corn, soybeans and small grain, produces some of the biggest bucks on the continent. Superior genetics, fertile soils and a great abundance of nutritious food are the reasons. Since cover, not food, is the limiting factor, deer populations vary according to available cover. Fair to good numbers exist where cover is sufficient.

Overall, pressure is moderate, but some areas are subjected to heavy pressure. Hunting pressure has taken a toll on the number and age of the mature bucks in some areas, but enough bucks live long enough to provide some of the finest giant buck hunting to be found.

Because of limited cover, the Midwest offers high huntability. Besides the Plains & Prairies region, which in many respects is very similar, I consider the Midwest to be perhaps the most huntable of all regions, at least when it comes to hunting an individual buck once he's located. Well-defined food sources, clear travel corridors and limited bedding options make patterning a buck just a little easier than in other regions. However, hunting the Midwest is not without its obstacles.

One of the main difficulties is that hunting is mostly on small tracts of land, usually from 150 to 500 acres, and bucks

might spend only part of their time on any given tract. This can limit access to big bucks and make patterning difficult. Also, short seasons, firearms restrictions and, in some cases, limited firearms seasons during the peak of rut act to swing the odds back in the buck's favor. All this means that seeing a big buck in the Midwest is not necessarily the problem; killing him might be.

The average mature buck in the Midwest scores an impressive 140 or so. There are plenty of 150s around, and 160s are a distinct possibility. Record-book bucks are there in numbers that only central Canada can match. Still, big bucks are not everywhere even in the Midwest. They are widely scattered among the many small farms, and unless you know that there's a big buck on the tract you're hunting, the Midwest can be frustrating. But for the serious hunter willing to do his homework and find a specific buck to hunt, there is absolutely no better place to shoot a 160-plus buck, or even a book deer for that matter. But because of the need to hunt a specific farm, as opposed to an area, and preferably even a specific buck, the resident hunter has a great advantage over the visiting hunter in the Midwest.

∽⌒ HOME ON THE RANGE ⌒∽

Depending on where you are in this region, you might know the Plains & Prairies for its endless wheat fields or shimmering grasslands or perhaps its stark sagebrush-studded landscape. To the Eastern hunter, this country doesn't look much like a place harboring big whitetails, but the fact is that the Plains & Prairies region is one of the better trophy whitetail areas in the U.S.

This region is unique in that its whitetail populations are largely confined to ribbons of habitat, namely riverbottoms and the associated fingers of cover. Often, fertile agricultural fields are adjacent to the riverbottoms to provide an abundant food source for the deer. Along these watercourses, deer densities can be among the highest anywhere, and overcrowding is a problem in many areas. Yet vast chunks of this region have few or no whitetails. The Plains & Prairies curve only reflects the riverbottom habitat.

The Plains & Prairies is one of the most huntable regions since the deer are largely confined to strips of cover. This is ranch country, and pressure, herd condition and habitat quality vary considerably from ranch to ranch. Overall, pressure is low to low-moderate, but even at that, high huntability has generally reduced the number of mature bucks present and the top-end size. Still, low pressure and high deer densities result in one of the highest localized populations of mature bucks to be found. For sheer numbers of mature bucks, only the famed ranches of Texas can compare with the better Plains & Prairie ranches.

The average mature buck scores around 130, and anything over 140 is a trophy. Bucks topping 150 are in fair abundance on the better ranches, and 160s are there but take

some hard looking. Despite some slippage in top-end size, book deer are shot there every year. Overall, the Plains & Prairies is one of the very best places to tag a 125 to 150 whitetail. I actually rank the better ranches there on par with the better ranches in South Texas, and where overcrowding is not a problem and hunting pressure is minimal, the top-end can be even better!

⚜ ROCKY MOUNTAIN HIGH ⚜

In this vast mountainous country, the bugle of elk fills the autumn mornings, grizzlies still roam the backcountry, moose forage the hidden beaver ponds, mule deer feed in the alpine meadows and the buffalo still roam ... right alongside big whitetails. This is the land of the great Rocky Mountains, and many of the valleys and associated hillsides are home to the whitetail.

I have chosen to combine both the Canadian and the U.S. Rockies in this region because the trophy prospects north and south of the border are essentially the same. Only the eastern front of the Alberta Rockies, where massive bucks typical of farmland Canada are sometimes shot, edges ahead of the overall trophy prospects of the rest of the region. Also, hunting quality tends to tail off as you move farther west into British Columbia and Washington and Oregon.

Hunting pressure is fairly low throughout the region, and, on average, deer populations are moderate. The average mature buck runs a very respectable 135. Bucks in the 150s are present in encouraging numbers, and I consider this size buck to be an achievable goal for the serious trophy hunter with a week or so to spare during the rut. A 160-plus is a realistic possibility, and record bucks are not uncommon. With the vast public holdings on the U.S. side, this area offers the best public land hunting for trophy whitetails in the country.

The one drawback in this region is its huntability. The expansive evergreen forests are not easy to hunt, especially for those new to the region. Deer populations tend to be somewhat localized, and figuring out what the deer are doing can be an intimidating experience when someone first tackles this rugged, inaccessible and sometimes inhospitable country. Only Eastern Canada and the North (U.S.) would be harder to hunt, but higher deer populations and lower hunting pressure make hunter success much higher here.

CENTRAL CANADA: COLD, HARD FACTS

Central Canada is a frigid, snow-covered land where the arena for a trophy hunt can be either great northern forests or small woodlots dotting expansive agricultural fields. The whitetails there are perhaps the biggest of the species. Low to moderate pressure, especially in "big bush" areas along the northern fringes of the farm country, allows many bucks to reach the necessary age to realize their great size potential. Harsh winters and predation from coyotes and wolves act to prevent overcrowding. In fact, deer populations are moderate at best and are downright low in many areas. Low deer densities coupled with poor logistics, restrictive laws, extreme cold and deer that lean toward nocturnal activity make central Canada a challenging place to hunt.

The moderate number of mature bucks is due to moderate at best deer populations. Though pressure tends to be low to moderate overall, some of the southern farm country gets hammered pretty hard, making mature bucks hard to find there. The number of mature bucks increases as pressure decreases and cover increases in the northern fringe country, where most nonresidents are legally forced to hunt.

You would think that these farm country bucks would be fairly easy to hunt, but that is not the case. They are very skittish and tend to be nocturnal. Also, they often cover long distances in their travels, especially during the rut, making locating even a known buck rather dicey. Interestingly, their big woods counterparts in the northern forest areas are much more apt to move around in daylight and are less nervous.

In areas where baiting is legal and practiced, namely upper Saskatchewan, I would describe huntability as fair. I can't rank it much better than that because the harsh weather and often poor logistics still make hunting very tough. Plus, mature bucks are not as easy to bait in as some would have you believe. Where baiting is not legal in Alberta and Manitoba, huntability is something less than fair, especially outside the rut. Limited daytime movement often requires that deer drives be employed.

On average, mature bucks score a whopping 140-plus in central Canada. They routinely top 150. Scores in the 160s are common for older bucks, i.e., those $5\frac{1}{2}$ and older. Record-class bucks are an ever-present possibility. In fact, I'm certain that a higher percentage of the mature bucks reach record-class proportions there than anywhere else in the world. The top-end is virtually unlimited, and world-class bucks are shot there every year. The only area that even compares to central Canada is the Midwest. No other place consistently turns out such massive antlers as this region. For giant whitetails, those over 160, I consider this region to be the best place going for the visiting hunter.

Of course, Saskatchewan is home to Milo Hanson's world record typical whitetail, which scored $213\frac{5}{8}$.

⇜ EASTERN CANADA ⇝

This region consists largely of vast wilderness forests more suited to moose than whitetails. Most deer are found where man's activities—farming, clearing and timbering—have replaced the comparatively sterile virgin forests with crops or regrowth that make life in the harsh land more bearable for the whitetail. The best deer hunting is around the scattered pockets of agriculture, found mostly along the U.S. border.

Deer numbers here range from fair around the border agricultural areas to downright disparaging in the more remote, less disturbed areas. For our purposes, we're only considering the areas along the border that have reasonable populations of deer. Happily, hunting pressure is light almost everywhere. Even so, the number of mature bucks is relatively low simply because deer densities are meager.

For reasons I've never fully understood, deer in this region do not reach the antler size (body sizes can be impressive there) of their U.S. counterparts just across the border. It must be a combination of the soil, genetics and perhaps weather—severe cold and deep snow. As you move farther east into the Maritime provinces, trophy size does increase once again, especially antler mass.

Mature bucks scoring about 130 are trophies. Bucks that top 140 are a reasonable hope only in the best agricultural areas. A 150-class buck is about as big as you can expect. But as the record book shows, Ontario has squeezed out six book bucks, so the region can hold a surprise or two.

Huntability depends on where you are in the region. In the big bush areas, finding a buck, let alone a trophy, can be more work and challenge than most hunters care to take on. In the farming areas, huntability can be fair to good, depending on the layout of the land and on hunting pressure. On balance, this is a difficult region to hunt. Couple that with low deer populations and limited size potential, and you can see why this region has captured little of the trophy hunting limelight.

In Conclusion

Lucky is the hunter who gets to experience hunting the whitetail in each of these regions. In a lifetime of hunting, few of us will do just that.

But it's always fun to dream, and what's wrong with making a trek to some new whitetail country to give the hunting a try? There are only so many autumns in a lifetime ... maybe this is the one you'll try to make that special trip you deserve.

This story gives you the basics you need to know to start turning your dreams into reality. Whitetail hunting close to home is fun, to be sure. But there's a lot more ground to cover in search of trophy bucks.

HOW THEY GET THERE

by David Morris

Many years ago during my early tenure as a bass guide on Georgia's Lake Eufaula, I learned a lesson that I've never forgotten. At the time, Eufaula was about the hottest big bass lake going. Six- and seven-pounders were commonplace, and eight-pounders hardly turned a regular's head. It took a nine-pound-plus fish to rate trophy status among the lake's hardcore.

THEY HAVE TO BE THERE

On this particular occasion, a couple of chaps from Arkansas had booked me for three days. When I met them at the marina late on the afternoon prior to our trip, I began to probe into their fishing prowess as soon as the niceties were dispensed with.

The first guy was in his late 30s and had the weather-worn look of a man who had spent many an hour under the hot sun having his hide tanned to leather. When I asked him if he fished much, he smiled confidently and said, "About 300 days a year. I'm a full-time guide on Lake Ouachita." The thought raced through my mind that I had to quit this line of work before my hide became as corrugated as his.

"What about you?" I asked his companion.

"Every weekend and holiday, and any other time I can get away from the plant," the athletic-looking 30-year-old said.

Now came the big question—the one I always asked to really size up a guy's fishing ability. In my mind, everything else I might learn about them was secondary. Now I'd find out what kind of fishermen they really were. "What's your biggest bass?" I asked with a certain note of finality.

"Seven pounds, 14 ounces," came the guide's response.

"Just under 7½," the younger man said proudly.

"Good fish," I responded patronizingly, having now placed them solidly in the "fair fishermen" category based upon their answers.

Well, over the next three days those "fair fishermen" took me to school on bass fishing. They fished circles around me. When the smoke cleared, they had both topped their previous personal record three or four times and had run up an enviable score on six- and seven-pound bass.

As they were preparing to return to Arkansas, one of them occasioned to say, "Great trip and a great lake! You can't catch fish like this at home. They just aren't there."

In that simple statement lies a profound truth that I've never forgotten. Nobody, no matter how good he is, can catch or kill something that isn't there! It's not a question of skill, knowledge or tactics. Those things only become factors in success when what you seek is present. And this truth applies just as well to trophy whitetails as to trophy bass.

HUNT WHERE THE BIG ONES ARE

Countless would-be trophy whitetail hunters go through the motions of hunting trophy bucks year after year and never shoot one for the very same reason that those Arkansas fishermen had never caught any really big bass. They are hunting something that is not there—or that exists in such low numbers as to make their chances of success practically nil. The only absolute prerequisite for killing a trophy whitetail is being where there are trophy whitetails! True, to take trophy bucks with any consistency, a hunter needs to have a high level of skill and knowledge, but he must hunt where such animals live in appreciable numbers!

Before proceeding, we need to distinguish between the terms "mature" and "trophy." We'll use the same standard outlined in "Are They Different?" found earlier in this chapter. "Mature" means any buck 3½ years old and older. "Trophy" is a mature buck big enough to rank among the better bucks consistently taken in an area. This definition requires that a trophy buck be at least 3½ years old and large relative only to the other bucks in that particular area; not necessarily large in absolute terms or in comparison to the bucks in a different location. Thus, our definition works anywhere and takes into account the inherent size differ-

---

"Every trophy hunter must decide for himself what size buck is big enough to meet his personal trophy standards."

---

ences from one area to another. Much of this discussion will focus on mature bucks since trophy bucks will be a natural by-product of a population of mature bucks.

Every trophy hunter must decide for himself what size buck is big enough to meet his personal trophy standards. Once this is done, he must then realistically evaluate his chances of meeting his standards where he hunts. Or he can reverse the process—first evaluate the trophy prospects where he hunts and then set his trophy standards based on the largest buck he feels he has a reasonable chance to take there. If the evaluation process leads a hunter to the conclusion that the size he is after is not available where he

Any quality herd will have an ample percentage of representative deer from varying age classes. Like father, like son.

Buck-to-doe ratio is an important ingredient in a location's potential to produce quality bucks. Too many does means too many deer. And that means an unhealthy situation.

hunts, he must search elsewhere and be able to calculate his odds there. Any way you look at it, a trophy hunter needs to be able to size up the trophy prospects where he plans to hunt. There are basically three major considerations in evaluating the trophy prospects of a place: The number of mature bucks present, their size and their huntability. These considerations are influenced by many factors, but no one factor has a greater influence on a given area's overall trophy prospects than hunting pressure. The relationship is simple: The greater the pressure, the poorer the trophy prospects.

How Many Mature Bucks?

The number of mature bucks present is of paramount concern in evaluating trophy prospects. The more mature bucks around, the greater your chances of shooting a trophy. Essentially, three factors contribute to the number of mature bucks. One, the density of the deer population. Two, the buck/doe ratio. And three, the buck age structure. The latter two are largely determined by hunting pressure. Let's look at each one.

Herd Density
All things being equal, greater deer densities should mean more mature bucks and greater odds of trophy success. It's simple arithmetic. For instance, if two tracts of land have similar buck/doe ratios and buck age structures but one tract has twice as many deer as the other, which

tract offers you the best chance of seeing a mature buck? The tract with twice as many deer offers you twice the odds!

On the other hand, herd density can be a two-sided coin for the trophy hunter. Too many deer means overpopulation, which reduces antler size due to poor nutrition. For the trophy hunter, the abundance of deer and where the herd stands relative to the carrying capacity of the land are

"Three factors contribute to the number of mature bucks: herd population density, buck/doe ratios and buck age structure."

both important concerns.

I generally consider herd density to be the least important of the three factors, but there are a few places where overall deer numbers are so low as to be only marginally huntable. Examples can be seen on the fringe of the whitetail's range in such places as the vast northern forests of Canada and parts of Mexico. Such extremely low populations are the exception, and ample numbers of deer exist just about everywhere whitetails are hunted.

The fact is that trophy hunting can be quite good even in relatively low populations. I would much rather hunt an

131

area with few deer and a tight buck/doe ratio and good buck age structure than a high-density herd with a disproportionate number of does and a depleted buck population.

Buck-to-Doe Ratio

One of the major ways in which hunting pressure impacts a deer herd is in the ratio of "adult" (1½ years old and older) bucks to adult does, known simply as the buck/doe ratio. Generally speaking, the buck/doe ratio is "higher" or "tighter," meaning more bucks in relation to does, in lightly hunted populations and "lower" or "wider" in heavily hunted herds, especially those with disproportionate pressure on bucks. Fawns are not included in the buck/doe ratio; therefore, the ratio between antlered and antlerless deer will reflect an even greater spread, sometimes nearly twice as much since a healthy herd can average close to a fawn per adult doe in the fall. As a result, a buck/doe ratio of, say, 1:3 could mean an antlered/antlerless ratio of around 1:6. Antlerless sightings could give the wrong impression of the buck/doe ratio without taking this into account.

The buck/doe ratio is simply a means of expressing the makeup of the adult deer herd. It can be easily translated into percentages. For instance, a buck/doe ratio of 1:1 means that 50 percent are bucks and 50 percent are does; a 1:2 translates into 33 percent bucks and 67 percent does; a 1:3 ratio results in 25 versus 75 percent, and so on. With this understanding, it is easy to see that the buck/doe ratio has a direct bearing on the number of bucks in the population.

Assuming a piece of property is capable of carrying only so many deer without sacrificing size, then it is obviously

Thick cover means a buck gets a better chance to grow old.

to the trophy hunter's advantage to have as many bucks represented in that population as possible. The lower the buck/doe ratio, the greater the percentage and the higher the total number of bucks present. And logic dictates that more bucks in a herd leads to a greater likelihood that mature bucks are present. As for does, it is only necessary to have enough to replenish the losses each year, assuming that the herd is at carrying capacity. A buck/doe ratio unnecessarily weighted toward does means space is occupied by does that could be filled by bucks.

Buck Age Structure

Unquestionably, the most damaging impact of hunting pressure on trophy prospects is seen in the buck age structure, which is simply the distribution of bucks throughout the various age classes. High hunting pressure results in fewer mature bucks and lower trophy prospects. Light hunting pressure assures the ample presence of mature bucks, greatly enhancing the trophy outlook. Age is, after all, the most limiting factor in trophy production across the country, and hunting pressure more than anything else will determine how many bucks survive to reach maturity.

Summarizing, the herd density determines the total number of deer present. The buck/doe ratio determines how many of the deer are bucks. The buck age structure determines how many of the bucks are mature, which translates directly into the number of trophies available.

GROWING TROPHIES

Let's now see how the three cornerstones of buck size—genetics, nutrition and age—figure into the trophy prospects of one particular area.

Genetics

Genetics determine the size potential of the bucks at any given age. The quality of nutrition determines how much of that size potential is actually realized at a given age. Last, but certainly not least in the equation, sufficient age is required for bucks to reach their maximum size under the existing genetic and nutritional realities.

Nutrition

In reality, the full size potential of bucks is seldom achieved. Most often, realization of the size potential is limited by inadequate nutrition, largely from overcrowding, and the lack of age, mainly due to hunting pressure. It is even possible for the natural genetic potential of a herd to be eroded through the heavy, long-term harvest of the better antlered bucks. The fact is that most of us can do little to change the existing genetic, nutritional and age status of a deer herd. While it is helpful to understand their roles, there is not much point in dwelling on the "potential" of a place (unless you are in a position to manage that place to better achieve full size potential). Rather, most trophy hunters are better served simply by determining the size of the mature bucks actually being taken in a given place, or put another way, how much of the potential is actually being realized.

To that end, there are a couple of aspects of interest.

—⟨ ⟩—

"Three cornerstones of buck size: genetics, nutrition and age."

—⟨ ⟩—

One, the average size of the mature bucks. Two, the range of sizes represented by the mature bucks within the herd. This second aspect, the size range, is a critical factor in determining the number of better-than-average mature bucks, i.e., trophy bucks and the realistic top end size. While nutrition and genetics play critical roles in the size attained by mature bucks at any particular location, the variable most often of foremost concern to trophy hunters is the buck age structure which, of course, is a function of hunting pressure. Let's take a closer look at how hunting pressure affects both the average size and range of sizes of mature bucks.

Age

In lightly hunted populations, bucks of all ages are present. In heavily pressured herds, relatively few bucks even reach maturity and bucks older than 3½ are downright rare. However, a buck is not as big at 3½ years old as he will be at 5½, 6½ or 7½ years old, normally considered peak antler years. It is easy to see that a population of bucks distributed throughout all the "mature" age classes, 3½ to 9½, will average older and bigger and will span a greater range of sizes than a population whose mature bucks are primarily 3½-year-olds. In a population with a well-distributed buck age structure, the top-end size will be greater because of the increased presence of peak-sized 5½-, 6½- and 7½-year-old bucks. It's simply a matter of more bucks reaching the age necessary to achieve their genetic potential under existing nutritional conditions.

Huntability

While trophy bucks must be present before a hunter has any hope of success, the hunter still has to be able to kill them. Even when the numbers are the same, the degree of difficulty in hunting trophy bucks, that is, their "huntability," varies from place to place. Buck huntability is a definite factor in sizing up the trophy prospects of a place, but it ranks well behind mature buck numbers and size in importance.

Sizing Up by Region

Most serious trophy hunters are well aware that great differences exist in the size of bucks, even those of the same age, from region to region across the country. Even under identical and ideal conditions, some places inherently produce relatively small deer; others grow medium-sized deer; and still others turn out large deer. This difference in size is where genetics and nutrition enter the picture ... and, as taxonomists would say, so do the subspecies differences. For the traveling hunter interested in hunting the biggest bucks available, the inherent difference in size from one place to another is an important consideration in his analysis of trophy prospects.

133

Many factors bear on buck huntability. For instance, timing of the season is a big one. If the hunting season fails to coincide with the rut, buck huntability is greatly reduced. Another factor is the herd density relative to the carrying capacity. In overcrowded herds, deer will concentrate on food sources and tend to move more during daylight hours because they have to feed longer and more often since quality food is in short supply. Access to hunting land and certainly the size of the properties that can be hunted by an individual also figure into huntability. Obviously, weather, moon phases and the like enter the picture, but these things have a temporary impact, and that impact is essentially the same from place to place. There are, however, two overriding variables affecting buck huntability that we'll focus on here. They are hunting pressure (there it is again) and habitat conditions.

HUNTING PRESSURE

Hunting pressure both suppresses and alters deer activity. The more pressure, the less daylight movement and the less predictability in deer patterns. Even rutting activity is suppressed by high pressure. Feeding patterns are affected to an even greater degree. The extent to which deer react to human pressure should not be underestimated. Normal movement patterns are easily disrupted, and the deer can become virtually nocturnal, especially trophy bucks.

Since the rut is such a critical part of trophy hunting, a closer look at how hunting pressure affects buck huntability during the rut is helpful. Besides the simple harassment factor, which in itself forces the deer to alter their patterns, hunting pressure brings structural and behavioral changes to the deer herd that are detrimental to rutting activity.

First, heavy pressure adversely impacts the buck age structure by reducing both the percentage and the actual number of mature bucks in a herd. Beyond the obvious harm done by reduced numbers, this results in a buck population made up largely of immature bucks that have not yet developed the competitiveness nor the rutting behavioral patterns (we'll discuss these later) characteristic of mature bucks. As a result, traditional rutting patterns and activities break down and the rut is fragmented, non-competitive and indistinct. Even the few mature bucks in such a population fail to establish clear rutting patterns since the natural structure of the herd has broken down.

Next, heavy pressure results in a wider buck/doe ratio, which further results in an indistinct, spread-out rut. The ready availability of does reduces the competition between bucks. Most of the breeding and rutting activity takes place at night. Daylight movement is spotty and unpredictable. Rutting sign is halfhearted and undependable. All in all, this situation makes for very tough trophy hunting.

By contrast, a tighter buck/doe ratio is accompanied by a more competitive rut. More of the ritual activities associated with the rut, which are of greater importance to the trophy hunter than the breeding per se, are played out in daylight hours as the bucks vie for dominance and the relatively limited supply of does. Bucks lay down more sign, and this sign can be hunted with some predictability. Bucks spend more time during this period preoccupied with the rut rather than survival. That spells opportunity for the trophy hunter.

HABITAT CONDITIONS

The huntability of the habitat is a key consideration independent of hunting pressure. Here, we're talking about how the characteristics of the country affect the huntability of bucks. There are some places that are just plain hard to hunt. Thick cover, rough terrain, swampy conditions, inaccessibility, unbroken tracts of uniform cover, etc., can reduce your odds even though the trophy bucks are there. Still, I much prefer tough hunting country with trophy bucks than easy country without big bucks!

IN CONCLUSION

The most skilled whitetail hunter in the world using the most deadly tactics ever devised will not kill a trophy whitetail where none exist. That being the case, the first thing a trophy hunter must do is accurately size up the trophy prospects where he hunts. Are trophy bucks present in huntable numbers? What size trophy is a realistic possibility? What are the real odds of success? Without the answers to these questions, you might be hunting something that simply is not there!

Confessions & Lessons from a Trophy Hunter

by Jim Shockey

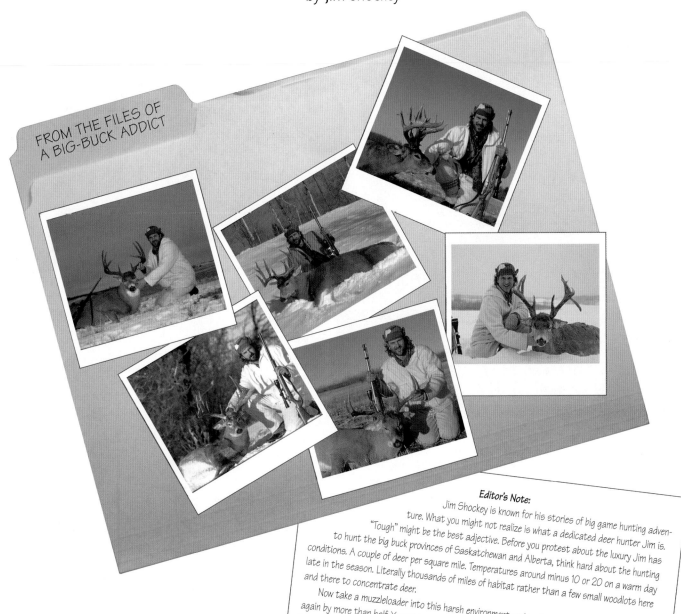

FROM THE FILES OF A BIG-BUCK ADDICT

Editor's Note:

Jim Shockey is known for his stories of big game hunting adventure. What you might not realize is what a dedicated deer hunter Jim is. "Tough" might be the best adjective. Before you protest about the luxury Jim has to hunt the big buck provinces of Saskatchewan and Alberta, think hard about the hunting conditions. A couple of deer per square mile. Temperatures around minus 10 or 20 on a warm day late in the season. Literally thousands of miles of habitat rather than a few small woodlots here and there to concentrate deer.

Now take a muzzleloader into this harsh environment and realize that you've cut your odds again by more than half. You might spend a full week on stand, daylight to darkness, to see one "good" buck. And it's quite possible you won't see any at all. We'd all love to have bucks of this caliber to our credit. And as you read the accounts of some of Jim's lessons taught by old whitetail bucks, it might appear on the surface to be rather easy in this land at the northern extreme of the whitetail's range. Don't kid yourself. For each of the successes comes a giant measure of sacrifice that could fill many more pages.

What follows is intended to give you some insights into what makes trophy whitetails tick.

— G.G.

135

A good buck spot is a good buck spot ... is a good buck spot. This reality spans time; it holds true not only from day to day during a single hunting season but from year to year. If I see a big white-tail buck in a given area once, I know if I hunt the area intensively enough, I'll see that buck again in that area.

Perhaps even more important, whatever caused the first buck to wander into that particular area—whatever combination of habitat, food, doe concentrations, weather or whim—I know the same combination of factors will cause another buck to wander by on another day. If I don't see the first buck again, I'll very likely see a different big buck.

The year before I killed this gnarly non-typical with my muzzleloader, I killed a big 5x5 in the exact same spot. That year, I hunted the area for two days, killed the buck and went home. A full year passed before I returned. No pre-season scouting, no inside information, no talking to the farmer, nothing but the belief that another good buck would be in the same area for the same reasons (whatever they were).

Mine was not to wonder why. It didn't matter; a buck would show. And show one did. At 10 a.m. on the first day, I spotted a beautiful 11-point buck. Long story short, I missed. As far as I know, that buck is still running.

Which brings us back to the lesson. That buck obviously wasn't coming back, and who would blame him! I'm sure there's something disconcerting about a 300-grain muzzle-loader slug slamming into the hill beside you. What to do? Look for a new hunting spot? Head for greener pastures?

Nope.

The very next morning, I was right back in the same stand. Wasn't I the vindicated one when at high noon, out walked this non-typical?

A good buck spot is a good buck spot ... is a good buck spot.

RATTLING RESULT

- Score: 167 $\frac{2}{8}$ net typical B&C
- Points: 5x5
- Shot distance: 15 yards running, straight on
- Rifle/load: .50 caliber Knight Magnum Elite/sabotted 300-grain lead alloy bullet, 100 grains Pyrodex Select powder
- When: Mid-November, rifle season

W hat now? That was the question I asked myself as I watched the magnificent buck make his way through the opening 350 yards away. With a centerfire rifle, the shot was a "gimme." A long "gimme" to be sure, but for all intents and purposes the buck would have been in the bag.

However, as is my choice, I wasn't using such a firearm; I was shooting my muzzleloader. If I was going to get a crack at the buck, either I was going to have to get closer to him or the buck was going to have to get closer to me. From his actions—head down and trotting away toward the heavy timber—the chance of me moving in closer was nil. The odds of him coming back closer to me were about the same. Unless …

For years I carried a pair of rattling antlers with me wherever I was hunting whitetails. In those years prior to seeing that giant buck, I'd rattled in a total of five bucks. Not a great endorsement for rattling as far as I was concerned. Still, I carried rattling antlers on the off chance that they might prove their worth some day. And if ever "someday" had arrived, it was right then.

I pulled the antlers from my shoulder, even as the buck disappeared into the forest. He suddenly wasn't a whole animal, becoming instead only a flicker in the trees—but still

enough of a flicker for me to see his reaction when I banged the antlers together. He stopped dead in his tracks!

Obviously he heard. Just as obviously, when I clanked the antlers together a second time, he was on his way. Truth be told, I had only enough time to drop the antlers, sit down and click the safety off before the enraged buck charged over a rise 15 yards away.

The lesson? The most difficult part of killing a big buck is seeing that buck. In the event that you can't take him when you first see him, don't ever give up. Try anything you can to get the shot. If the buck hadn't come to rattling antlers, I wouldn't have given up, I'd have gone after him. Yes, the odds would have been long, but not as long as trying to find another buck such as he.

CLOSER THAN YOU THINK

- Score: 160 B&C
- Points: 6x4
- Shot distance: 80 yards
- Rifle/load: Knight DISC/sabotted 300-grain Barnes X-bullet, two 50-grain Pyrodex pellets for powder
- When: Early December, rifle season

Drop-tine bucks are rare.

So naturally, when I overheard some local scuttlebutt about a drop-tine buck living in a couple-square-mile patch of bush, I decided to investigate. This buck, I soon learned, wasn't a "one-hit wonder." He'd been seen by several different people during the summer and early fall. When I uncovered this information, I was confident that I'd get a poke at him. As far as I was concerned, he was living right where everyone had seen him.

I just as quickly learned that I was alone in this belief. During the first four weeks of the hunting season, several groups of hunters had tried and failed to find and kill the buck. As hunters are wont to do, when the buck wasn't killed, everyone assumed he'd moved somewhere else for the hunting season and wasn't living where he'd been for the previous few months.

Stubborn might not always be a favorable character trait in the everyday world, but during whitetail season it sure is. I ignored the nay-sayers and set up my spotting scope on the highest point in the buck's domain. From my vantage, I could see most of the clearings and fields for a mile in every direction. As it turned out, my wait wasn't long.

The very first morning I set up, I caught the buck sneaking across a frozen swamp, back into the big timber. I tried unsuccessfully to waylay him in the next clearing, misjudging the distance by a couple hundred yards, and had to let him pass. Instead of giving up, I took his track for the rest of that day and the next.

It was a merry chase to be sure. Round and round he went, always one step ahead of where I could have seen him. Interestingly, not once did he leave the two-square-mile main area he'd been living in all summer. By day three, he'd involuntarily taught me his ways well enough for me to take an educated guess as to where he'd be the next day.

As it turned out, he was exactly where I expected he'd be. I knew his tracks well by then and, within minutes of legal light, came across his fresh, long-toed prints and extra-long strides. This time, instead of following, I headed on a course that would take me on a circuitous route, around where I figured he would have bedded.

Two hours later, almost at the exact spot where I'd first crossed the track, the buck jumped up from his bed. It's hard to say whether he was watching his back-trail, expecting me to be following him as I'd done for two days, but it sure appeared to be that way.

The big old buck never ran when he jumped up, he just stood still at the very edge of my vision. Unfortunately for him, I found a shooting lane and squeezed off a shot. The drop-tine buck that was supposed to have moved out of the country died within 100 yards of where he'd been sighted more than a dozen times by the local townsfolk.

The lesson? The buck is still there. Believe it and don't give up. He's there all right, and if you spend enough time in the area, you'll bump into him.

FATHER KNOWS BEST

- Score: 140-plus B&C, 24 inches wide, typical
- Points: 5x5
- Shot distance: 100 yards
- Rifle/load: Knight DISC/ sabotted 300-grain Barnes X-bullet, two 50-grain Pyrodex pellets for powder
- When: Early December, rifle season

Unfortunately, there are times when the lesson comes after you are tagged up. Such was the case with this buck. I was shooting a new video and was playing a figurative game of Russian roulette. Time was running out, and I was having to do some serious soul searching every time I turned down a buck that would have made for great video footage.

In fact, I played the game for two weeks and turned down several special bucks in the hopes of capturing a real big one on camera. It wasn't until the third-to-last day that I pulled the pin on this 24-inch-wide 5x5. Certainly an excellent and respectable buck but not as large as others in that area.

Tagged up, I called my 71-year-old father to come out and hunt. I mentioned that I'd turned down a few good bucks and that he, a meat hunter, should be able to take a buck in a day or so. He drove up, and the very next morning we were on stand together with the cameras rolling. Luckily, my father slept through the first couple small bucks or I'd have had a tough time keeping him from shooting. To his credit, he did wake up when we changed stand locations.

We weren't in our new position for an hour when his buck came walking out. As soon as I saw the buck, I realized that it was one I'd turned down (four different times in two weeks, we found out later when we reviewed the video footage). Calm as the veteran deer hunter that he is, my father popped the cap on my Knight muzzleloader, placing the bullet perfectly. The buck ran 50 yards before expiring.

So what's the lesson I learned after I was tagged up? Well, it turned out that the buck my father killed—the same one I'd turned down several times—was significantly larger than the one I took! If I would have known just how large, I would have certainly pulled the pin on the buck the very first time I laid eyes on him. I learned that no matter how "expert" you think you are at judging whitetails, there is no sure way of knowing how big the buck is unless you pull the trigger and put your hands on his antlers.

NOCTURNAL? NOT!

- Score: 168-plus B&C non-typical
- Points: 5x4
- Shot distance: 120 yards
- Rifle/load: Knight Magnum Elite/sabotted 300-grain lead alloy bullets, 100 grains Pyrodex Select powder
- When: Mid-November, rifle season

Ask most whitetail hunters about big bucks and they'll tell you that "big bucks are nocturnal." To that I say "bull wiggle!" Big bucks aren't nearly so nocturnal as they are "bushternal." The hunters who use the roads as their trails have created a whole new breed of white-tailed bucks that won't show their faces in the open during daylight hours, but that doesn't mean that they're nocturnal.

Now granted, I'm fortunate to be able to hunt in some vast areas of solid bush, and I can usually hunt at least one mile from the nearest road. But vast area or not, the hunting pressure along the roadways is intense. The interesting thing is, in 10 years of hunting where I hunt, I've never once come across another human's footprints! Yet in that same time back in the bush, I've come across literally dozens of "supposed-to-be-nocturnal" bucks walking around in broad daylight!

This was one such buck. He walked right up to where I was standing in an old burn. At 50 yards, I squeezed the trigger. Click. Again I cocked and squeezed and again there was no sound but the sickening "click" of a misfire. I tried a third

time with the same results.

The buck watched my performance, shocked, I believe, that there was a human so far back in the forest. After the third misfire, I remembered dropping the caps in the snow the day before. So I dug frantically in my possibles bag looking for some fresh caps. I eventually found them and just as quickly found the buck in my scope again. He was retiring to a less noisy part of the forest, but wasn't leaving in a big rush. At least not in a big enough rush to keep him off my dinner table.

The lesson? Get off the beaten track. Get back in the woods as deep as you can get and you'll find those "nocturnal" bucks everyone hunting along the roads can't find.

CREATIVE ADAPTABILITY

- Score: 174-plus B&C typical
- Points: 6x7
- Shot distance: 80 yards
- Rifle/load: Knight MK-85/sabotted 300-grain lead alloy bullet, 100-grains Pyrodex Select powder
- When: Mid-November, in a shotgun or muzzle-loader-only hunting zone

*I*f there is one phrase that I believe describes the best whitetail hunters, it would be "creative adaptability." They do whatever is necessary, within the letter of the law, to get the buck.

I spotted this particular buck early one morning as he followed a doe into the timber. It was bitter cold, and the snow was covered in a thick crusting of ice that turned every step into a noisy affair and still-hunting into a debacle. There was no way a hunter could slip quietly through the forest.

On the other hand, I didn't think I had to slip quietly, I only had to slip along in a way that would sound like a buck walking. To this end, I removed my felt pac boots and separated the outer-leathers from the inner-liners. Then I pulled the felt-liners back on. Once I was back on my "make do" moccasined feet, I started walking through the forest on my tip-toes. I'd like to say that I sounded like a deer, and likely I did, because I found the buck and his doe standing, waiting for me several hours later.

Whitetail bucks don't play by rules. They don't behave in a certain way because the books say they do. And to be a good whitetail hunter, neither should you. Throw a curve ball once in a while, try something that isn't "usual." Adapt to every hunting situation creatively and you'll greatly increase your odds of bringing home your biggest buck ever.

Unkillable Bucks: Do They Exist?

by Greg Miller

*I*t was one of those sights that every serious white-tailed deer hunter hopes to experience at least once in his lifetime. Approximately 100 yards straight out in front of me in a winter-flattened alfalfa field, I spotted the matched shed antlers of a huge buck. Even though I was alone on that early-April day, and even though I knew that the sheds certainly weren't going anywhere, I still found myself running full-speed toward the bony treasures.

The excitement I felt upon first spying the sheds was nearly overwhelming. But it didn't compare to the feelings I experienced when I reached down and grabbed those antlers. Six evenly matched typical points sprouted from each heavy beam. In addition, there were three non-typical points on the left antler and one odd point on the right. After figuring in what I considered a conservative inside spread, I estimated the 16-point sheds would end up taping close to 170 inches. (Which they did.)

Although more than a half-dozen years have gone by since I found that set of sheds, I still recall with perfect clarity what I did after picking them up. Taking an antler in each hand, I shook them at a distant wooded bluff and hollered out a promise to the buck that had dropped them. I would spend as much time as it took to figure out exactly where he was sleeping, exactly where he was eating and exactly where he preferred to walk when traveling about his home range. I would find him!

Now, I'd like nothing more than to continue on with an exciting story of how I worked my tail off and eventually managed to ambush the big buck. Unfortunately, it didn't happen. In fact, as far as I know, I didn't even come close. Even though I hunted the area quite hard (but very carefully) over the next three seasons, I never caught so much as a glimpse of the monster deer. But to be perfectly honest, I really didn't expect that I would. That's because I'd already had more than my share of experiences with these special creatures.

ELUSIVE BUCKS: UNKILLABLE?

The special creatures I'm referring to are unkillable bucks. In case you haven't guessed by now, I fully believe that such critters exist. I'd like to add that this belief isn't based on mere assumption or off-handed speculation, either. I've actually done a fair amount of non-scientific research on the subject. And while I don't have volumes of paperwork or stacks of fully-loaded computer disks to document that research, I do have hundreds of hours of personal observation and dozens of first-hand experiences to back up my claim. Trust me: Unkillable bucks exist wherever whitetails are found.

And just what do I consider to be an "unkillable" buck? Basically, it's a deer that manages continually to evade even the most dedicated and knowledgeable hunters out there. Regardless of what sort of well-planned hunting strategies are employed, these special animals always seem to stay at least one step ahead of their pursuers. To be honest, just getting a glimpse of an unkillable buck should be considered a major accomplishment.

Veteran Illinois deer hunter Stan Potts has taken more than a dozen Pope and Young Club bucks. He also has harvested two others that qualify for the Boone and Crockett Club's record book. Such impressive credentials make it obvious that Potts thoroughly understands mature buck behavior.

"I fully agree that unkillable bucks exist," he told me recently. "It's my opinion that these deer are able to constantly dodge hunters because they behave in a totally different manner. It could be that they've developed these special survival skills because of numerous past experiences with hunters."

He's been rutting, he's tired ... but he's still not a pushover.

PURE PRESSURE

While I believe there are a number of factors that can help create unkillable bucks, hunting pressure certainly ranks at the top of the list. Let's face it. Whitetail bucks that reside in heavily hunted areas must learn rather quickly how to become masters of evasion. And any buck that manages to survive three seasons in such an area is well on his way to taking on the characteristics that will make him "unkillable."

This isn't to say, however, that it takes bucks that live in lightly hunted areas longer to develop survivalist-type mentalities. In truth, bucks that are exposed to very little human intrusion often develop highly reclusive lifestyles at a very young age. A perfect example of this type of deer behavior can be found in most big woods environments. Remember, unlike their farmland cousins, wilderness whitetails have very little or no contact with humans for much of the year. Because of this, it's not unusual for big woods bucks to slip into totally nocturnal movement patterns at the first hint of human activity. As we all know, nocturnal bucks are virtually unkillable.

I've had scores of experiences with nocturnal buck behavior, but a big woods buck that I hunted some years back stands out most vividly in my mind. The monster deer taunted me by continuing to make fresh rubs and scrapes all

Either side of night—and midday itself—are the best times to see a truly big buck.

over his core area throughout the pre-rut. Unfortunately, all this activity was occurring after dark. Thinking that the buck would surely become daylight-active once the rut kicked in, I continued to hunt him hard. I finally realized, however, that not even the alluring odor of an estrous doe could draw him out of his daytime sanctuary. (I'll talk more about this later.) This truly was an unkillable buck.

"Those deer blessed with naturally skittish and reclusive attitudes certainly stand a much better chance of succumbing to natural causes than to a bullet or an arrow."

CHARACTER TRAITS, OR NATURE OR NURTURE?

Another factor that can have a tremendous bearing on whether or not a specific deer might eventually make it into the unkillable category is individual buck temperament. Personally, I've long believed that all white-tailed bucks possess their own unique personalities and temperaments. And it only stands to reason that those deer blessed with naturally skittish and reclusive attitudes certainly stand a much better chance of succumbing to natural causes than to a bullet or an arrow.

I've had many experiences that reinforce my beliefs about the individual buck temperament theory, but one I had several years back best illustrates my point. I was sitting on a treestand situated in a grove of acorn-laden red oaks when two yearling bucks walked into view. Their bodies were the same size and both possessed small racks with six typical points. But that's where the similarities between the bucks ended.

One of the bucks appeared quite carefree and almost oblivious to his surroundings. He'd feed on acorns for minutes at a time, never once raising his head to look around for signs of potential danger. Also, I don't remember seeing the deer ever stick his nose in the air to scent-check for predatory threats. It also seemed as though he was totally ignorant of the many suspicious sounds in the woods that afternoon. Judging from his behavior, it was highly doubtful that the buck would survive past opening day of the upcoming firearms deer season.

The other young buck, however, displayed a noticeably different temperament. Like his sibling, he too was feeding on acorns. But instead of becoming completely absorbed with the tasty little nuts, the buck would pick up a single acorn, then snap his head erect and slowly scan the woods

One of these bucks may, in future years, "drop out" and not partake in the rut. He will miss the action but save his hide!

around him. In addition, he was constantly testing the wind currents for the slightest whiff of a foreign odor. And several times after hearing suspicious sounds, the buck trotted off into some thicker brush. He'd then stand in this thick brush, studying his surroundings for many minutes before venturing back out into the open oak woodlot to feed. He finally spooked for good at the sound of a vehicle on a distant country road.

I believe the behavior displayed by the second of these bucks made him a likely future candidate for the unkillable category. It would appear that some whitetails are born with such temperaments. Potts agrees wholeheartedly with me on this matter.

"There's absolutely no doubt in my mind that each buck has his own unique personality," Potts says. "I also believe that a buck's personality plays a huge role in whether or not he will survive to that magical five-year-old age class. In my opinion, once a buck gets to be five years old, he's going to be darn near impossible to kill, regardless of what sort of environment he lives in. It's that simple."

PERSISTENCE PAYS

I should add that I've actually managed to harvest a couple of big bucks that I had originally deemed "unkillable." One of these deer, a bruiser big woods 11-pointer, led me on a chase that spanned the better part of two full seasons. Almost unbelievably, after making a fool of me for nearly two years, the buck then made what would have to be con-

sidered a "rookie mistake." He wandered out of his daytime hideout for a bite to eat at 9:30 a.m. I just happened to be sitting on a treestand that overlooked his favorite in-woods feeding area.

The scenario was much the same with the other "unkillable" buck that I eventually harvested. For two years the monster non-typical had successfully evaded my best efforts. Even though he continually confirmed his presence by leaving behind scores of huge antler rubs and numerous large hoof prints on the farm where I was hunting him, I never once actually saw the big deer. That is, not until late in the afternoon on a cold December day. For some reason, the once "unkillable" 18-pointer picked that day to walk out into a snow-covered alfalfa field a full 40 minutes before dark. Once again, I just happened to be in the right place at the right time.

So if I had already hung the "unkillable" label on these bucks, why was I still dedicating some of my very precious time to them? Well, call me crazy, but I always allot at least a little time to bucks that I consider unkillable. Of course, I fully realize that my chances of seeing those deer are quite slim. On the other hand, I realize that there's always a chance that a buck I've labeled "unkillable" will make a wrong move. The only way I can fully satisfy my curiosity is by occasionally hunting the deer.

SOME BUCKS DON'T RUT

No doubt some of you are raising an eyebrow or in some

The sanctuary—a place where bucks can go to escape human intrusion completely—is critical to growing trophy bucks.

other way displaying skepticism at my claim that unkillable bucks exist. I'd be willing to wager that your skepticism stems from a basic belief you have about whitetail buck behavior during the rut. According to your reasoning, there isn't a buck on the face of this earth that will totally ignore the enticing odor of an estrous doe. Even the most mature bucks in a given area will sacrifice their safety in an attempt to procreate. The way you see it, any buck that gets involved in the breeding ritual certainly is killable!

But I've got a bit of news for the hunters who believe that all bucks participate in the rut. They don't! This bit of information isn't based on a hunch either. Rather, it's based on sound research. That research, done by animal behaviorist Valerius Geist from the University of Calgary, Alberta, shows that some bucks actually go out of their way to avoid rut activity. According to Geist, "Non-breeding bucks aren't interested in the least in things like estrus odors or the sounds of other bucks fighting, either. Therefore, hunters will be wasting their time if they attempt to lure in one of these deer through the use of artificial estrus scents or by calling."

Like others, I once believed that old age was the major reason whitetail bucks become non-breeders. But this isn't always the case. "Some bucks actually develop into non-breeders at a very young age," Geist says. "This usually happens because of bad experiences they have while they're still quite young. For example, during our rut some years back I saw a young buck take a tremendous beating from an older, much larger buck. That beating obviously left quite an

impression on the younger buck. I kept close track of him, and he didn't participate in the rut at all for the next four years, even though he did grow to be a tremendous animal."

THE SANCTUARY FACTOR

One more thing that can figure into the unkillable equation is something I call the *sanctuary factor*. Regardless of where they live, whitetail bucks almost always have a place they can go that offers them total escape from human intrusion. Big woods deer can find safety and solitude in swamps or expansive regrowth areas. Farmland trophies can effectively evade hunters by moving into standing cornfields or by taking up residency on property that is off limits to any kind of hunting. (There are getting to be more areas like this every year). And suburban bucks seem to know that they can easily avoid hunters by moving deeper into residential areas.

I believe that hunters might not know how to recognize when they've taken up pursuit of one of these special creatures. In that regard, *is* there a fool-proof system for knowing whether you might be wasting your time on a particular buck? As far as I know, there isn't. But if you put in enough time, you'll probably cross paths with a whitetail like this at some point in your hunting career. Even if he wins, as most often is the case, you'll emerge a wiser hunter for the effort. And you'll probably be even *more* captivated by the whitetail's well-earned mystique.

146

TROPHY TALK

by David Morris

The keys to success on big bucks are simple: hunt where trophy bucks live and know enough about whitetail movement patterns to be able to predict what trophy bucks are likely to be doing before you ever step foot in the woods.

Let's again put these two elements in perspective. If your aim is to shoot a trophy buck, the most important step you can take toward success is to search out and hunt places that have appreciable numbers of what you're looking for. This is the very foundation of consistent success, and if you build your deer hunting strategy on any foundation other than that, you will be destined for failure. It's an inescapable fact that nobody can kill something that's not there. Skill, experience, hunting tactics, perseverance and even luck only become factors in success if what you're after is actually walking around out there. Even then, you still might not kill

your trophy, but if you don't hunt where he lives, I guarantee you won't get him!

Equally as important, though, is learning more about the tendencies of trophy bucks, especially in relation to the movement and travel patterns before, during and after the all-important rut. Buck behavior and travel during the fall follow predictable big picture patterns that are so dependably repeated from year to year that you can actually know in advance what trophy bucks are likely to be doing at a given time under a given set of circumstances. That's the beauty of understanding the basic biology of the animal and his behavioral patterns—you can hunt anywhere, anytime and, after doing some on-site homework, closely predict what the deer are likely to be doing, where they're doing it, and what tactics will work. Aside from the "where factor," I don't know what could be more important to success than this.

Now, one final note. This chapter has focused on hunting trophy bucks. We've defined a trophy buck according to the objective perspective of the total universe of deer hunters—namely, a trophy is a mature buck, at least 3½ years old, that is among the largest consistently taken in an area. That leaves room for place-to-place size differences and even some latitude for case-by-case judgment calls as to what is and is not a trophy. But frankly, when it gets right down to it, I still like the subjective individual definition that says "a trophy is a prized memento of one's personal accomplishment."

You see, I do believe "trophy" is in the eyes of the beholder. If a hunter is proud of his buck, regardless of the size, nobody has the right to say that deer is not a trophy. I have become sensitive to this in recent years as trophy hunting has increased in popularity and the term "trophy" has become more synonymous with "really big." As a result, a type of trophy snobbery has crept into our ranks. If a buck doesn't meet the standards of the trophy snob, both the hunter and his game are belittled—perhaps in mean-spirited terms or more often in subtle, condescending ways. Regardless of how, it's wrong, and I believe it is detrimental to the sport since it tends to especially discourage and even demoralize the young and inexperienced, who must eventually carry the hunting banner. And in case you haven't looked around lately, we hunters need all the folks we can get to line up on our side. This issue is fresh on my mind because I just saw a textbook case played out.

I was speaking to kids in the local school about, of all things, whitetail hunting (only in Montana!), and I asked who had taken a deer the past season. Several hands went up. Then I asked, foolishly perhaps, if anyone had killed a trophy. One 12-year-old kid who I knew well raised his hand high; in fact, he practically came out of his seat, a smile etched across his face. "I did! I did!" he shouted.

An adult, who prided himself on being an accomplished trophy hunter, responded in a patronizing voice, "Sit down, Joe. Your buck was just a nice eight-pointer, not a trophy."

I felt ashamed of asking the question and, in a way, of being a trophy hunter. I remembered the unbridled pride I had when I shot my first buck, which wasn't nearly as big as Joe's, and I thought about how I would have felt if someone had told me he wasn't a trophy. I walked over to Joe, who looked completely deflated, and as I gave him a 'high five,' I said, "Congratulations on a great trophy! It took me 10 years of hard hunting to kill a buck like yours."

Joe beamed with pride. So did I!

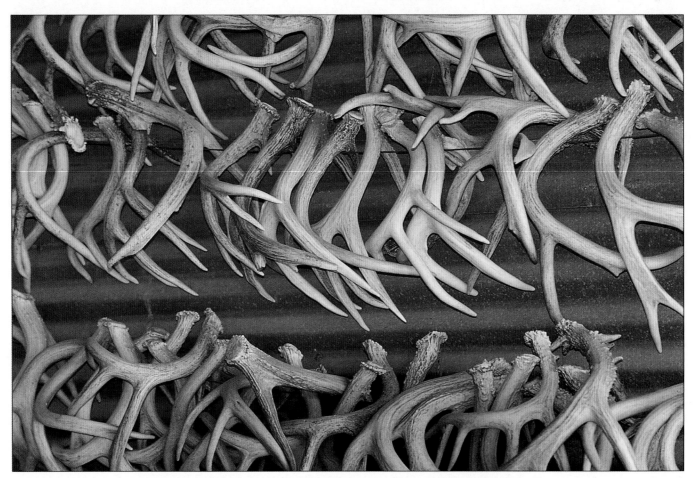

There's a special allure about antlers of all types. But piles of whitetail antlers cause many to gawk helplessly.

Real Trophies

Morris speaks the truth. Every deer is a trophy—no matter how many inches of antler it sports, or if it even has antlers at all. The most important record book is the one in your mind. How can a tally of inches compare with: the sunrise you saw that morning; the surge of your heart when that deer came into view; the satisfaction of know-ing all your hard work, preparation and effort came together perfectly; and the memories you forever savor from that day? Every deer is special. Here's a tribute to that: a collection of NAHC members with some very special deer—some big, some small, some without antlers but each a real trophy. You can tell by the smiles.

Christy Thompson-Texas

Mickey Fenn and Kevin Wisnaes - Virginia

Bruce Bennett - Alberta

Nicholas and Dave Fielders - New York

Sammy Wray - Indiana

Raymond Stevens - Maine

Sammy Wray says it best regarding his Indiana buck: "This is my first buck in fourteen years! Too long. He's not huge, but man is he a trophy in my heart!"

Dominick Orlando and Joey - Wisconsin

Kevin Mulkearn - Saskatchewan

Jack Krisanda (r) - New York

Bob Dinse - Michigan

Tom Carpenter - Minnesota

Andy Cashdollar - Illinois

Chapter 5

PERSISTENCE PAYS

Bill Winke said it best when he described in Chapter 3 how he visualizes the meter running during deer season. Successfully hunting white-tailed deer, as you'll read more about in this chapter, depends to a large degree on dedication.

Dedication without knowledge and a feel for whitetail behavior might be wasted energy in some cases. But the odds are still good for the deer hunter who logs the hours. Even if he or she doesn't sit statue-still on stand all day or toots on a grunt call too often, being out there where the whitetails live is necessary. "You can't shoot one in camp," the old saying goes.

So true, yet such difficult words to heed. If you didn't know it already, deer hunting is hard work. It is hot-cold-mosquito-rain-snow-wind-tired-dark tough … at least if you have come to the point in your deer hunting life where you have aspirations of attaching your tag to a mature buck.

Through the first four chapters of this book, you've read a few anecdotes of successful hunts that might make it seem easy for these fellows. Erase that idea from your mind. For all those hunts that end as we dream, there are hundreds of hours of wrong stands, wrong weather and wrong decisions. And there's what you need to lock away as you head to the deer woods next season: time counts.

It counts at least as much as—maybe more than—all the rest of the stuff tucked away in your daypack. It's as important as a quiet bow or an accurate rifle. And it's what makes the minute when that buck steps into range so captivating …

ONE STEP AHEAD

by Judd Cooney

Scouting is a year-round endeavor that takes place before, during and after the hunting season. Aggressive scouting—and utilizing the knowledge gained—can often make the difference between the success or failure of your whitetail hunt.

This fact was driven home for the umpteenth time during a bowhunt one early September in northern Montana. This hunt was set up by Bill Jordan, designer of Realtree Camouflage, and his right-hand man, David Blanton.

The main group of bowhunters would be hunting the grain and alfalfa fields along the Milk River on a series of adjoining ranches that had been under trophy deer management for several years. These ranches were producing some impressive whitetail bucks and equally awe-inspiring numbers of deer.

Harold Knight of Knight and Hale Game Calls, an equally avid bowhunter, and I would be bowhunting another ranch, on Frenchman Creek, with outfitter Don Lynn, owner of Montana Breaks Outfitters of Malta, Montana. Don has been in the outfitting business for many years, concentrating mainly on mule deer and elk. This was his first year at serious whitetail outfitting for bowhunters, but he was enthusiastic and had been doing his homework and scouting. Don had leased a mile section of land along Frenchman Creek that had a super population of whitetails including some real wallhangers. This choice chunk of prime Western whitetail habitat consisted of a series of irrigated lush alfalfa and barley fields surrounded by dense brush, impenetrable willow thickets and head-high grass and brush, interspersed with cottonwood, elm and alder groves (see diagram on page 153). The country surrounding the half-mile-wide riverbottom was open, barren, rolling hills covered with sparse sagebrush and coarse prairie grasses. The major portion of whitetail population there was concentrated along the riverbottom while mule deer roamed the open prairies above.

Don, along with head guide Eric Korman, had spent a number of mornings and evenings scouting and glassing the alfalfa and barley fields along the creek, pinpointing the location of some of the larger bucks and noting their entrance and exit routes from the bedding areas. Once they had determined where the bigger bucks were moving from the bedding areas to the feeding fields, they went in during the middle of the day and put up a couple of treestands to accommodate Harold and me for our hunt.

With the preferred whitetail habitat limited to the confines of the river- and creekbottoms of Montana, many deer populations tend to be

The arena for Cooney's Montana hunt ... where stands were juggled to keep that precious one step ahead.

Take the time to search out all your options before committing to a stand site.

very concentrated with a lot of deer moving, feeding and bedding in a small area. This high concentration of animals makes on-the-ground scouting and moving around without spooking deer a tough proposition.

THE HUNT BEGINS

The evening we arrived, Harold, Don and I drove to some high ridges a half-mile above the riverbottom, overlooking the area we were to hunt the following evening. In the hour before darkness, we glassed more than 100 head of deer feeding in the alfalfa and barley fields. All of the deer on the eastern edge of the riverbottom—where Harold's perch for the following evening was located—passed on the heavily used trails within bow range of his treestand. The distance and fading light made it impossible to see just where the deer were emerging on the far side of the field, where I would be waiting in ambush the next evening, but the sheer number of deer appearing in an endless procession out of the brush definitely got our adrenaline pumping.

The battle plan on all the ranch properties was to confine

our hunts to evenings only. Getting into the areas for a morning hunt without spooking or alerting the deer was almost an impossibility, especially where Harold and I would be hunting. The first evening, Don dropped Harold and one of Bill's cameramen off near his treestand in a gnarled old cottonwood at the outside curve of the meandering creek. All the trails leading from the brushy bedding areas, scattered for half a mile up the creek, merged into one major deer travel corridor 20 yards out from the cottonwood.

My stand was situated 15 feet up another cottonwood 30 yards in from the edge of a barley field where the barley had been cut and windrowed just a couple of days earlier. The stand overlooked a well-used trail down a narrow funnel of cover between the steep creek bank and the edge of the barley field that led to the outer perimeter of a green alfalfa field. An ideal setup.

At 6:20 p.m. a doe and fawn sauntered under my stand and gave me a chance to practice drawing a time or two. At 6:40 p.m. a Pope and Young-class eight-point buck appeared, moving slowly through the heavy grass and brush 50 yards from my stand. I watched as he moved out of the trees and

154

into another small barley field 100 yards from me and started munching barley heads. I had only given the field a cursory glance through the trees, but with my glasses on the feeding buck, I could plainly see that there was a 30-yard strip of barley still standing. Over the next couple of hours I watched deer after deer moving to and from that strip of uncut barley. Unfortunately, none of them came under my treestand. It was obvious that the deer had changed their travel patterns. When Don and Eric had glassed the uncut barley fields, the deer were using the barley and alfalfa with equal gusto and traveling the trail under the treestand to get to both feeding

---

"Getting into the areas for a morning hunt without spooking or alerting the deer was almost an impossibility."

---

areas. All might have stayed equal if the rancher had cut *all* the barley. But by leaving a narrow strip of standing grain to tantalize and attract the deer, he had totally changed their travel patterns.

THE STAND MOVES

Rather than being dejected when Don picked me up that night, I was hyped! I couldn't wait until the midday lull the next day so we could get back and confirm what my tree-stand scouting had indicated. The little patch of uncut barley would concentrate the deer in a smaller area and just might draw a big buck within bow range. The following day, Don and I circled the barley field several times in his pickup, checking trails, tracks and wind direction before I picked a spot for my stand. The end of the field adjacent to the thick brush and woods had five beaten-down trails emerging within the 50-yard width of the field and would have made an excellent stand location, but a westerly wind would have been blowing scent back into the bedding area. I finally put up a 14-foot ladder stand near the center of a strip of trees separating two of the barley patches where I saw a number of deer moving between the fields. The predicted northwest wind would be carrying my scent over the least likely travel area for approaching deer, and with the sun heating the field all day, there was a good chance that the thermal updraft from the warm ground during the cool evening would carry my scent up and out of reach of any nearby deer.

By 5 p.m. I was comfortably situated in my stand and ready for action. The first little buck ran into the field at 6 p.m. and literally attacked the standing barley. From that point until dark there was a constant stream of deer moving

into the field and past my stand. At one time there were 20 deer in the field feeding with nine bucks ranging from spikes to a wide-antlered nine-point that would have easily made P&Y. The larger buck, still in full velvet, fed to within 15 yards of my stand and posed broadside for five minutes before moving off. I passed, hoping for a bigger buck and knowing that this hotspot was going to do nothing but get

If things aren't working, move your stand!

155

better. By dark it was obvious that I needed to move my stand another 50 yards toward the end of the field into a huge cottonwood on a small point that protruded out into the field. Some of the deer were feeding up to that point and then meandering through the trees into the adjacent fields. From my present stand, I couldn't see the end of the field around the corner from the big cottonwoods, and I figured I might be missing some deer. From the cottonwood I could cover the whole lower end of the field and any deer that tried to move around the point.

THE STAND MOVES—II

Several of the hunters in camp had taken good bucks that evening, so the following day, Realtree's Mike Waddell, Don and I returned to the field at midday and moved the stand again. As with almost any whitetail hunt, just about the time you think you are getting ahead of the game and gaining an advantage, along comes something or somebody to upset the apple cart. In this case it was the rancher driving his trusty windrower. Had this been my lease, I would have already made arrangements with the landowner to leave a portion of the field as a food plot. This was a tactic unfamiliar to Don, and he didn't want to press the issue with the rancher right at that moment. By the time the rancher was finished with

the small plot of barley, our double stands were in place and we left to wait for evening. I figured the deer would return in numbers again that night since they were programmed to

"By dark it was obvious that I needed to move my stand another 50 yards toward the end of the field."

the standing barley, but once they found the barley cut they would start spreading out again.

By dark that evening I could have arrowed a number of smaller bucks in the 100- to 125-class and had seen one good buck in the 150-class on the far side of the creek. I decided to give that stand one more evening on the off chance the big buck would move across the creek and join the 25 or so that we had observed. When Don left earlier in the afternoon, he jokingly pointed out a small patch of uncut barley that the farmer had missed behind a dirt bank and stated, "See, he did leave you a food plot!" Every deer that came into the cut field that night ended up spending a few minutes munching in that small patch and presented me with a good shot. (Don't overlook small patches of choice feed because the deer darn sure won't.)

The following afternoon found Michael and me back in the same stand once again, but I didn't have very high hopes of lots of four-footed company. Since the barley fields were now all down and windrowed, there was nothing special to hold the deer in our field or bring them past my stand. I was right! That evening we had one buck come within bow range of the stand. Although we saw about the same number of deer, they simply scattered throughout the field we were watching and into the adjoining fields.

A few minutes before final shooting light faded, a very nice buck that would have scored in the 130s stepped out of the brush at the end of the field and worked his way along the edge of an irrigation ditch 50 yards across the field. He was a heavy-beamed eight-point with long tines

Versatility, portability and flexibility ... keys to whitetail hunting success everywhere.

and a perfectly matched rack. I would have taken him in a heartbeat had he been a bit closer and in better light. His appearance left no doubt about where I was going to move the stand for the last evening of my bowhunt.

The Last Stand

The following afternoon Mike, Don and I once again pulled the stands and moved to the end of the field. I eased into the heavy grass, brush and trees and carefully glassed the area for our last stand. Fortunately, the wind had shifted to the south and southeast, which gave us a lot more leeway in choosing a stand site. One heavy trail snaked along the bank of the creek that paralleled the bedding area for several hundred yards while the most heavily used trail was about 40 yards farther into the brush. As the main trails approached the field they forked and re-forked into numerous small trails. I found a suitable cottonwood right on top of the most heavily trodden trail where I could cover the two main trails and still have a pretty decent shot at any deer passing through the brush to the south. The southeast wind would give me a good shot at any passing deer before they had even a slight chance of winding us.

"I found a suitable cottonwood where I could cover the two main trails and still have a pretty decent shot at any deer passing through the brush to the south."

Both Michael and I wore scent-lock suits under our camo to help keep our scent to a minimum. I also sprayed the area around the base of the tree with scent eliminator. Though I don't think anything will completely eliminate or cover human scent under hunting conditions, even if our precautions only diluted our scent a bit it was worth the effort.

From 6:30 p.m. on, it seemed there was always a deer or two in sight, and several small bucks passed within easy bow range on both sides of the stand. The same wide-antlered eight-point and two does appeared, moving down the trail along the creek and somehow picking up a trace of scent on the wind. They showed alarm but bounded back the way they came without blowing and making a lot of racket. A few minutes later another nine-point came down the main trail and ended up right at the base of the ladder stand for five minutes, checking out all the strange smells before joining a couple of passing does and heading for the fields.

Quitting time was fast approaching—along with the end of my Montana hunt—when I spotted a buck coming out of a thicket 100 yards up the trail. I eased my bow into position for a shot and then saw that he was just a basket-racked eight-point. Out of the corner of my eye, I saw him veer off the trail and pause broadside at 25 yards. Now I picked up movement where he had appeared a few minutes earlier. Immediately, I caught the white flash of antlers—big antlers! I hissed to catch Mike's attention, and when I turned back the buck was coming at a trot. He veered off the trail at the same point where the smaller buck had. When he emerged from under the drooping branches of a low-growing cottonwood and I got a good look at his high rack, there was no doubt about my taking the shot. I jerked my 83-pound Bear bow to full draw and was about to halt the buck with a grunt when he stopped in the same spot as the smaller buck. My concentration was already centered on his rib cage, and the second he came to a stop my arrow was in flight. There was a flat smack and the buck was gone.

I don't believe in waiting the standard 30 minutes because all that does is give an animal time to start recovering. So I unsnapped my safety belt and was on the ground with my bow in less than a minute. The 10-point, 140-inch buck had made it through a small opening in the brush and was down for the count less than 15 yards from where my arrow had slammed into him.

Now that's the way to end a hunt! If I had just sat in my original treestand enjoying the scenery and patiently waiting for a big buck to wander my way, I doubt I would have come off this hunt with anything more than memories. By keeping my eyes open (scouting) and constantly trying to figure out what the deer were doing and why, I was able to move into a position where I was in the same place at the same time as a record-book buck. It might have only been for a total of a single minute or two over a period of five days, but it was long enough to take a trophy buck, and that's the name of the game.

HUNTING ALL DAY

by Bill Winke

I parked my truck at 11:30 a.m. that day and grabbed my bow, a treestand and my fanny pack full of tree steps. It was only a 20-minute walk across private land to the edge of the big chunk of public land beyond it. I had walked through this area quickly the spring before and had seen some very impressive rubs along a stand of pine trees just inside the public ground. I was headed toward that spot.

Since it was the first of November, I knew the rut would be getting into gear. The big rubs were there again and very fresh. I was hoping that the big buck that made them would make a trip along the edge of the pines sometime during the evening hunt. I just didn't expect him so soon.

I was still climbing the tree with my stand when I heard him coming. He came chugging up the steep bluff breathing hard with his mouth hanging open. It seemed he had already been on the move for most of the day. He was a 10-pointer in the 140-class, a buck that I would have been sorely tempted to shoot even though it was still early in the rut. But that was entirely academic as there was no way I'd be getting a shot with my bow lying on the ground! He passed 10 yards from the tree and disappeared over a rise, never slowing and never even glancing my way.

"Some of the most profitable time you can spend on stand occurs during the middle of the day."

Three days later, a much bigger buck caught me in another compromising situation, and again it was in the middle of the day. The giant eight-pointer would have scored in the 150s, no question. I was just reaching down for the tote rope to pull my bow up when he came crunching into view. I tried several times to get the bow off the ground, but the buck just got too close too fast. Soon he was right under me. Seeing the bow and then me, he bounded off 80 yards and stopped to look back at a sobbing hunter.

Not all of my midday encounters have ended in disappointment. In fact, several trophies have found their way onto my wall after showing up near my stand during times when most other hunters were getting lunch or taking a high noon siesta. Some of the most profitable time you can spend on stand occurs during the middle of the day, especially during the rut—and even more so when the weather is cool. If you aren't out there from dawn until dark during the best part of the season, you're missing a good percentage of the day's action.

Being out there at high noon can really pay off. The key is sticking it out.

WHY IT'S WORTH IT

Let's follow a good buck through a typical day during the rut. Our boy spends the night nosing around in the places where does feed. He paces from one of these areas to another looking for a doe in heat. Usually, shortly after daybreak, he'll follow a group of does out of their feeding area into the cover. Within an hour or two the does will all bed, and if none are close to their estrus peak, he'll quickly lose interest and be on the move again. His course might take him to another bedding area or to a hot scrape or two located in areas where does pass after leaving the fields. This second shift rotation corresponds with late morning, when most hunters are growing impatient, hungry or cold and have started filtering out of the woods.

Now let's look at the rest of the buck's day. Let's assume that he finds no amorous does. He will soon bed down for a short nap, probably in one of the areas he's checking, or, if he is old and wary, he will likely withdraw to somewhere more secluded. After a couple of hours of much needed sleep, the buck is up again, rechecking some of the same areas he hit earlier. Maybe he'll touch up a scrape or two and nose around a few more bedding areas. Finally, as sunset begins to spur the doe herd into movement, our buck drifts back to the feeding areas and starts the process all over again.

—————

"When buck movement is primarily nocturnal, you will do well to be on stand at midday."

—————

Another set of conditions can also produce a flurry of midday activity. At certain times, buck movement is almost strictly nocturnal. When this is caused by clear nights with a full moon, midday activity is often intensified. It seems as if every buck is up and walking for a short time late in the morning. This was the case on a recent rifle hunt at the Encinitos Ranch in South Texas. Despite the fact that the rut was heating up, daytime buck movement had slowly diminished with each day following a cold front. I saw 20 to 25 does on the third morning but not a single buck. This was especially perplexing since the ranch is managed for a 1-to-1.8 buck-to-doe ratio. I should have seen many bucks.

The first antlers appeared at 10 a.m., precisely when my guide stopped to check on me. We quickly resumed the hunt, and within 30 minutes I had a nice 10-pointer on the ground. Even as we drove back to the ranch an hour later, we were still seeing good bucks on the move. When buck movement is primarily nocturnal, you will do well to be on stand at midday.

LUNCH-TIME LOCATIONS

Just because you are on stand all day doesn't mean you'll experience action all day long. Certain types of travel routes produce better during the day than others. Stands located between bedding and feeding areas are distinctly different from those located between two bedding areas. During most times of the year, stands on travel routes between two bedding areas would be dead, but during the rut these are the places to find maximum midday movement. It's been my experience that you'll see fewer bucks on bedding-to-feeding trails during the early phases of the rut than on travel routes between two (or more) bedding areas. While hunting bedding-to-bedding buck travel corridors I see many bucks, but rarely a doe. However, most of the time these areas go completely dead about an hour before sunset and take at least an hour to heat up in the morning. By their nature, most of these stands are also in areas that will allow me to access them easily without the risk of spooking deer before first light or when leaving after dark.

Basically, you are looking for stand sites that are located in any type of funnel between two heavily used bedding areas. Also, in areas with broken terrain I try to find a topographical feature that I know bucks will use in a predictable manner. Funnels offer the best bet for action. The ideal bedding-to-bedding stand site is located back in the woods where little exposure is required for the oldest, smartest bucks to move about. Even the less secure, more exposed travel routes, such as a fenceline, are often used at midday in areas where hunting pressure is light.

You won't find a lot of buck sign along bedding-to-bedding travel corridors because bucks only use them to get from point A to point B and they don't mess around much along the way. You'll almost never find a trail—maybe some kicked-up leaves if you're lucky—so don't be fooled by the lack of sign. Trust your instincts and set up a stand. At first you might feel silly, but the bucks you see thereafter will keep you on the edge of your fold-out seat for entire days at a time.

One nice feature of midday travel routes is their ease of access. They are not near feeding areas, which means that you can get to and from them in the dark without educating any deer. As long as the wind blows your scent into areas that don't contain deer during the day, your stand will permit almost surgical precision and efficiency.

MIDDAY STORIES

Here are a couple examples of midday bedding-to-bedding stand sites that have worked well for me in the past.

One of my favorites is a stand that I have in a wooded fenceline between a cornfield and a large patch of idle farmland field. It connects three wooded points with a 200-acre woodlot. Deer, of course, bed heavily on these wooded points, and the woodlot serves as home for eight to 10 more does. As long as the wind blows my scent out into one of the fields, I almost never have a deer catch me on stand. I shot a dandy there several years ago, three hours before sunset.

Another classic stand that I've used several times overlooks a large rock quarry. The quarry cuts deep into the side of a gradual slope, leaving just 100 yards of cover between

Bedding-to-Feeding Travel Routes

Travel routes located between bedding and feeding areas can produce fast action on bucks during the rut, but it often takes place at sunrise and sunset. Getting to and from these stands without spooking deer is the hardest part.

its top lip and the field edge above. Any deer traveling the sidehill between the bedding areas on either side of the quarry must pass through the funnel on top, often within bow range and always within gun range. I only hunt the spot when the wind is carrying my scent out over the quarry. I can climb up the slope along the quarry's edge to get into my stand completely undetected. That stand has produced plenty of midday action through the years.

TOUGHING IT OUT

Seeing the effectiveness of midday hunting and actually staying out there all day are two different matters. Spending the whole day on one stand is very tedious business. Just a couple of days of this type of hunting can drive me crazy. I remember a hunt I went on in Manitoba several years ago. It was the last week of October and it was starting to get cold in the Interlake region. I spent four and a half days sitting from dawn until dusk before I saw the only buck of the trip. I had seen a grand total of three does prior to that. I spent every daylight minute of my six-day hunt on stand. By the time I got back to the Midwest I was too burned out even to think about hunting ... at least for a couple of days!

If you don't have the patience to sit all day on one stand—and few hunters do— then consider moving to a different stand late in the morning. This can break up the monotony and give stiff muscles a chance to

——⟳⟳⟳——

"If you don't have the patience to sit all day on one stand, consider moving to a different stand late in the morning."

——⟳⟳⟳——

loosen up. It is also a great time to spot-check for buck sign around a couple of other stands for future reference. Just don't delay too long because good action might be passing you by.

Dressing properly is one key to staying out there all day. (See "Dressing for the Cold" on page 110.)

Bedding-to-Bedding Travel Routes

Midday during the rut, bucks are likely to use travel routes that connect two doe bedding areas. Here's an illustration one of the author's favorite daytime stand setups, utilizing a "natural" funnel between two doe bedding areas.

If you're going to stay out all day, you're going to have to eat. Bring plenty of food, and make it good for you.

The right clothing for maximum warmth will help you stay out there for extended periods. I have a few tips that have worked well for me. Find a good pair of loose-fitting insulated bib overalls with zip-up leg openings. Carry these, along with your other outerwear, when walking to your stand. This will keep you from sweating which will, in turn, help you stay much warmer once you get settled. You can pull the overalls easily over your boots once you get to your destination. Tie-on hand muffs are great for keeping your hands warm. Dry, air-activated handwarmers can be used in many ways—including sandwiched between two inner clothing layers—to keep you cozy. Eat a well-balanced breakfast and carry a good lunch with you. Just as a

motor requires fuel to run, your body burns calories to keep you warm.

Persistence is one of the most critical qualities that a would-be trophy hunter must cultivate. Always keep in mind that with big bucks, it only takes one deer to change your whole season. A big buck can show up at any time. You might be sitting on stand, convinced that there isn't a good buck within miles, and 10 seconds later you could be drawing your bow or shouldering your gun on the biggest buck you've ever seen. Time spent on good stands is what it's all about, and every minute on stand brings you one minute closer to seeing a big buck.

WHEN A PLAN COMES TOGETHER

by Bill Winke

A few years ago, I enjoyed a hunt that produced a giant buck and brought to light many of the things I've learned over the years. It serves as a good example of how the process of persistent hunting works from start to finish.

I was hunting a new area that season. It was a large block of ground that holds a lot of deer and some really good bucks. Years of searching for the best possible areas within my home state of Iowa had brought me to this particular farm. I did only two days of scouting during the spring, with only a couple of stands going up as a result. As the bow season rolled around, I was just one step removed from going in cold. Due to heavy spring rains, only two crop fields had been planted on the property; both were in soybeans. In early October, I began hunting one of those fields.

ON THE FOOD PATTERN

I started by hanging back on the downwind edge to get a look at what was coming out and where. The second evening, I slipped into a better position. From there I saw several bucks, but a couple of them really caught my eye. They were both dandies—bucks that would push Boone and Crockett Club minimums. I immediately began hunting those two deer.

Regardless of where they came out, it seemed as if all the bucks were passing within bow range of several trees that jutted out from the edge of the woods. The next evening I moved closer to those trees, but high winds kept the deer under wraps. The tension grew as the week rolled on. I was able to hunt the stand several more times without seeing either of the two bucks. Finally satisfied that I had things

Big bucks have a tendency to move right at the edge of daylight. If you can't see your sight pins clearly through your peep, that rare chance might slip away.

pretty well figured out, I moved to a tree that offered the best possible chance for getting a shot should one of the bruisers come out. It had taken me five evenings to narrow it down, but now I was ready.

First Chance

Three evenings later I got my chance. Twenty minutes before sunset, the does began to gather in a grassy area next to the woods' edge. If events followed the normal routine, the does would munch on the clipped hay grass for awhile and then line out past my stand and into the bean field. Any bucks that came out would eventually follow them. I only hoped one of the giants would be among them.

The wind had been good all evening, but now it began to blow from the woods straight out into the field. The does would have to pass directly downwind of me on their way to feed. I held my breath as the first group of six does started to pass. They were close, and I hoped my scent would blow over their heads. I guess they weren't close enough. Catching a whiff of my scent, the lead doe jumped and stiff-legged it back toward the rest of the group. Soon all the does and fawns in the grassy opening were watching the nervous doe. As long as she didn't blow I was still all right.

One of the giant bucks picked that exact moment to step out of the woods and begin cropping grass. He was more than 100 yards away, but my binoculars revealed each long tine on his wide, 10-point rack. He paid little attention to the does despite their tense body language. Soon he was joined by several lesser bucks. Now I had three distinct

groups of deer waiting to pass my tree. They were strung out for 125 yards down the narrow strip of short grass. It reminded me of jets lined up in the queue for landing at Chicago O'Hare. There was plenty of daylight left. This still has a chance, I thought.

The first group of does again started heading carefully toward my scent stream. I had done everything possible to eliminate my scent. I only hoped it would be enough. Again, the lead doe locked up and turned back. This time she stamped the ground and blew loudly. Now she had everyone's undivided attention, including the big buck's. The group milled for another 15 minutes. During that entire time the big buck never once took his eyes off the doe.

Obviously, she hadn't gotten a real strong hit of my scent—or maybe the beans were just too tempting. With only five minutes of shooting time remaining, she again began heading my way. Just as before, she hit the scent stream and froze, only this time she bounded forward instead of back, taking the whole group with her. This was the signal the second group of does had been waiting for. They immediately lined out and walked briskly past my tree, not showing any signs of scenting me. Seventy-five yards behind the does, the big buck was now coming my way at a steady walk!

With only minutes of legal time remaining, the buck began to pass through the narrow shooting lane, where I waited for him at full draw. The 20-yard shot should have been a piece of cake. I was excited, but not overly. Why can't I get the pin on him, I thought?

When I focused on the buck I couldn't see my sight pin, and when I focused on the pins I couldn't clearly see the buck. The whole time he was walking slowly through my shooting lane, perfectly broadside. My peep sight had cut down the amount of light that reached my eye; what should have been an easy shot had turned into a five-second nightmare. As I focused on the 20-yard pin, I saw movement enter the peep sight from the direction the buck was approaching. It was now or never. I punched the trigger. "THWACK."

"Now she had everyone's undivided attention, including the big buck's."

Why wasn't the buck running? It never occurred to me that I might miss. In fact it took several seconds before the realization struck home. He stood there perfectly broadside in my shooting lane, staring up at me. He hadn't been scratched! I had blown it! Scrambling, I tried to get another arrow on the string before the buck got away. I never made it. Even as I came to full draw he was stiff-legging out of my

166

Travel Routes During the Rut

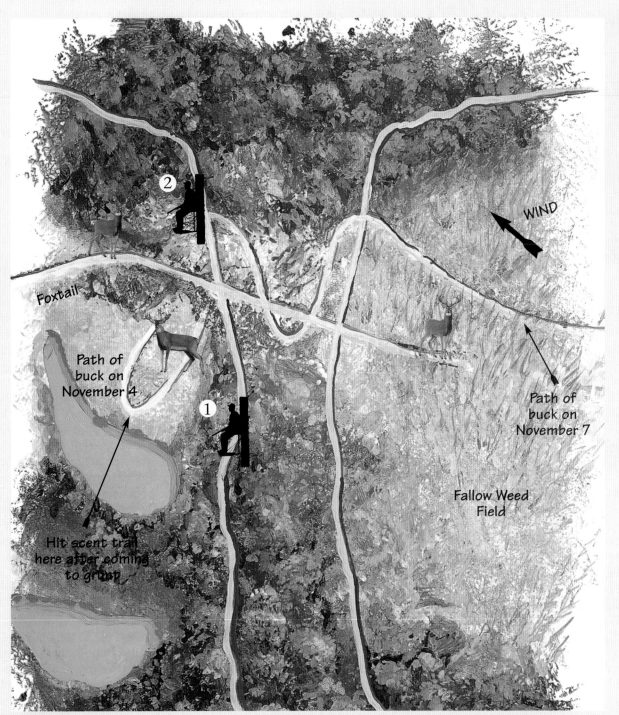

The buck was first seen from Stand 1. At that point, he came almost all the way to the grunt before smelling the author's scent in the tall foxtail grass. Three days later, the buck was arrowed from Stand 2. He was following a doe through the bottleneck of this travel route.

Author Bill Winke with a great Iowa whitetail earned through persistence and attention to detail.

shooting lane. For several days after I kicked myself until I was finally able to resolve things.

My mistake had been glaring. I had always shot at walking bucks without trying to stop them, reasoning that when they stopped they might not be exactly in one of my typically narrow shooting lanes. With the light fading fast, I should have whistled or grunted to hold him as I took the needed time to get everything lined up. There had been enough light for a *good* shot but not enough for a *quick* one.

TRAVEL ROUTES

My next real action came two weeks later after hunting several days in Illinois and then returning to the soybean field.

The day dawned clear, cold and still with lots of frost. It was the perfect morning for every buck on the property to be moving. By 9:15 a.m. I had seen several bucks, including a 140-class 10-pointer and something bigger that I couldn't clearly make out. Both had been out of range and did nothing more than stop momentarily to look in my direction when I grunted at them.

I was beginning to think about climbing down when I saw a buck standing along the edge of the woods about 150 yards away. He had plenty of mass, but his head was down and I couldn't tell anything about his tines. He wasn't overly wide, either. I wasn't even sure he was a keeper until he raised his head and looked to the side. My eyes must have doubled in size as the binoculars clearly revealed a wall of long tines on each thick beam.

Up until then I had been fairly detached, but now I was tearing at my chest pocket for the grunt call. With my heart racing, I watched for a few moments to see which direction he would go before I called. His first step was away from me. "Uuurrrp." Nothing. It would need to be louder. "URRRRPP!" He stopped and looked my way. Another softer grunt got him started. He came walking slowly along the edge of the trees, heading straight for my stand. I was absolutely confident that I had him. (By now I should know better than to think that way!)

"My eyes must have doubled in size as the binoculars clearly revealed a wall of long tines on each thick beam. "

Still 75 yards away, the buck began to circle out into the chest high foxtail grass that grew in the small field in front of me. That was okay. He would still be forced by a thin line of brush across the field to come within 25 yards. The wind was perfect. Things looked great until the buck hit my entry trail. I had slipped through the foxtail that morning believing the center of the field to be the least likely place that a buck would approach from. Surely he would work along the edge of the thin band of trees. Wrong!

He locked up for only 10 to 15 seconds before blowing loudly and bolting 50 yards in the opposite direction. He stopped, and steam issued from his nostrils as he blew again. By the time he was out of sight I was sick.

After continuing to work the area around the bean field for two more days, I again decided to try the long finger of brush. I pulled out my aerial photos at noon on the 6th of November and chose a spot about 400 yards from where the buck had hit my scent trail two days earlier. I knew that the wind would be perfect for the spot the next morning, so I quickly sneaked in and put up a stand. Leaving the spot, I went back to the bean field that evening.

SECOND CHANCE

Daybreak on November 7 found me 20 feet off the ground watching the long finger. I planned to stay on stand all day. Much like it had the previous time I hunted this area, the day dawned cool, crisp and frosty. I hadn't been on the stand more than 10 minutes when I heard the distinct sound of a buck grunting and saw a form dashing along the far side of the finger. Directly opposite me, probably only 30 yards away, the buck stopped and peered intently into the cover. I couldn't make out antlers yet and didn't want to risk pulling my binoculars up. After a few moments, the buck put his head down and dove into the cover, crashing back in the direction he had come.

I knew from his behavior that the buck was intercepting a doe that was trying to use the finger to get to a large block of connected timber 100 yards beyond my stand. Does usually win such contests eventually, so I expected to see that buck again. Twenty minutes later, right after the start of legal shooting time, I saw the doe coming straight down the middle of the finger. I didn't move as first one buck, and then a second, showed up 30 yards behind her. The first buck was a 130s eight-pointer, and the second was much bigger. I didn't try to size him up; one glance told me he was better than big enough. It appeared as if the doe would bring him right past me for an easy shot.

It took only two seconds for everything to unravel. The doe turned from her ideal course and then stopped right under my stand. I'm sure she could smell my ground scent. Worried by the smaller buck and beyond the point of caring about the doe's body language, the big buck charged forward. Both the doe and the smaller buck bounded out into the CRP grass on my side of the finger. The bigger buck, in turn, stopped right where the doe had been—directly under my stand. I can only assume that he smelled my scent, but that he was on my right side now—with me sitting—was a much more pressing emergency.

It seemed as if deer were crashing everywhere as I literally jumped to my feet and tried to draw my bow on the buck. For some reason, I couldn't get to full draw. I pulled back harder with my right elbow. No way! Suddenly my release arm shot forward and the arrow rattled against the bow. Surprisingly, the arrow didn't come off the string. The buck was still there, but with ears cupped my way, he was starting to walk warily out into the grass.

Fearing that something had gone wrong with my equipment, I quickly unclipped the release aid, removed the arrow, replaced it, rotated the peep sight, reattached the release and this time came easily to full draw. The buck was still within range, 25 yards out and angling way from me, walking parallel to the edge of the woods.

Remembering the low-light lesson I'd learned in October, I grunted loudly with my mouth to stop the buck for the shot. He took one more step and then froze—right behind the branches of a fallen tree. So much for stopping a walking buck! I looked for an opening but found none. Within seconds the buck was moving again. Briefly, I considered grunting a second time but ditched the notion as I pulled my barely visible sight pins ahead of him.

FINALLY, THE SHOT

Hurriedly, I guessed the range at 30 yards. When the correct pin settled on the buck's shoulder, I punched the release. "THUP." It sounded like I'd shot a watermelon. The buck's first reaction was to kick up his hind legs before busting through the finger of cover. Everything suggested a good vital hit, but as I replayed the shot in my mind, I began to suspect that the hit could have been several inches back from where I had planned. At worst, I figured I had struck liver—a very deadly hit but one that you can't push.

I simply sat down in the tree and waited four hours. Surveying the situation more closely, I noticed the large limb that had prevented my elbow from fully extending on the straight-down shot. A couple more nice bucks passed my tree as I relaxed and ate an early lunch. By the time I climbed down from the stand, I was confident that the buck was dead somewhere close by.

—◦/◦/◦—

"He took one more step and then froze—right behind the branches of a fallen tree. So much for stopping a walking buck!"

—◦/◦/◦—

The blood trail was light and washed out by the melted frost. I easily followed the deep, running tracks as they angled 100 yards across the band of cover to the opposite edge. A large fallow field of shoulder-high weeds bordered the woods on that side, limiting visibility. I stood at the last blood and searched intently on the ground nearby. At one point, I thought I smelled a buck, but I dismissed the thought. Finally, I began glancing farther out and was shocked to find that I was practically standing on him! Fifteen yards away I could see a heavy antler sticking above the short grass that grew under the overhanging limbs. There were six long points on it! I had killed the same giant buck that had come part way to my grunt call three days before!

STRATEGY SUMMARY

I adopted a low-impact strategy that kept me out of the big wooded areas on the farm. No doubt, these blocks of cover served as bedding areas and major rutting hubs. I had no intention of messing up such places. By staying out, I was able to keep the sensitive areas fresh while I waited along the fringe travel routes for something good to happen. It did, in a big way!

RULES ARE MEANT TO BE BROKEN

by John Wootters

*I*n order to have any lasting value, this book will have to give a hunter who reads it something to think about. This is more important, in fact, than actually teaching something that the hunter didn't know before. Hunting the North American white-tailed deer in fair chase is, perhaps surprisingly, a quite cerebral pastime. A big game hunter can climb to a Rocky Mountain goat, walk to a mule deer or pay the way to a record-book elk ... but a hunter thinks his way to a big, mature white-tailed buck.

We hear a lot about "luck" in whitetail hunting—how this hunter got lucky on the new state record or that one had beginner's luck on a book deer. I'll tell you a secret: The longer I study the whitetail scene, the more I'm tempted to conclude that luck is something invented by losers to explain the success of those who are better than they are at whatever is being discussed! Beginner's luck is often a matter of an inexperienced hunter making, through ignorance, exactly the right—and often unorthodox— move at just the right time, which is not quite the same thing. Hunters who consistently fill their tags with old bucks year after year are not lucky; they're good, and they're hunting good places. There's very little luck, in the sense of blind good fortune, in deer hunting.

Furthermore, the white-tailed

deer might be the only species of North American big game for which the mere expenditure of money, energy and time cannot guarantee a record-book trophy, at least in a truly fair-chase context. More than any other, this species demands a fourth ingredient: knowledge.

Successful whitetail hunting is usually not physically demanding, as hunting mountain game can be, but it is nevertheless hard work. Not only does it require a great deal of patience and time in scouting and setting up, one has to think a lot ... and thinking is some of the hardest work there is! The greatest asset a deer hunter has is not a firearm or camouflage or a bait pile, but the unique power of the creative imagination!

Every extraordinarily successful whitetail hunter in my long experience has been a person of imagination. None of them took the white-tailed deer for granted (which is very easy to do ... and easy to regret) and none of them ever allowed the deer to take them for granted. Without exception, these legendary hunters have evolved their own distinctive theories of whitetail behavior and tactics for whitetail hunting. They read and listened politely to so-called experts, then went out and asked the deer, learning from the only real experts on whitetail behavior: the animals themselves.

These hunters do things differently, by building on the experience of those who taught them and pushing the envelope for themselves, experimenting with new approaches and ideas. Their techniques never cease to evolve because these hunters never cease to challenge their own assumptions. They haunt the woods, always watching and wondering, noticing details about the whitetail lifestyle and trying to find new fits between observations and orthodoxy. Where they

cannot, all the legendary hunters I've known have thrown out the orthodoxy and boldly proceeded on their own novel concepts.

In my own extensive writing and lecturing about hunting the wily whitetail, I've always stressed this: We might not be very successful in "patterning" the buck, but we must at all costs prevent bucks from patterning us! That means pitching the buck a curve, a woodlands change-up, playing it a different tune, showing it something that it hasn't seen before. It's all too easy to get locked into a hunting rut, doing everything the way our grandfather or uncle always did it. That's not only obsolescent, it's boring, and whitetail hunting should never be boring!

Therefore, I welcome innovation in the deer hunting scene. In recent years alone, the introduction of serious grunt-calling and the use of decoys, to name just a couple of tactics, have greatly livened up my hours in the woods. My present opinions on these two subjects are today almost opposite to my earliest reactions to them.

On the other hand, it's all too easy to get caught up with gimmicks and gadgets. Whitetail hunters are no more immune to these diseases than golfers or bass fishermen. Some new products are actually useful, and some are fun, but none can replace a thorough, basic understanding of the white-tailed deer and the world in which it lives. Gadgets are like icing on a cake, but they can never substitute for a hunter's skill and knowledge. The most successful deer hunter will always be the person who knows most about the animal's needs, priorities, character, habits and responses. That's why this book is important to anyone who wants to be a whitetail hunter.

The slightest glimmer of just one new idea—perhaps based on something that has been said in these pages—can revolutionize your whole approach to deer hunting.

Author John Wootters and a beautiful Texas buck.

INDEX